How to Listen with Intention:

The Foundation of True Connection, Communication, and Relationships

By Patrick King
Social Interaction and Conversation Coach at
www.PatrickKingConsulting.com

Table of Contents

Chapter 1. One Mouth but Two Ears

Picture someone visiting a new therapist or counselor, and the dialogue they have in their first session. The client is, quite naturally, feeling a little nervous and exposed, and is trying to find their feet—this is the first time they've done anything like this, and they're not quite sure about how it all works. Are they going to lie down on a couch and be asked about their attraction to their mother or father? Will they uncover something traumatic from their past that they have blocked out?

They come into the room and the therapist invites them to sit. The client sits and eventually the therapist invites them to talk, saying, "So, what's brought you here today?"

"Well, it's hard to say, actually," says the client, who starts describing how they want to use therapy as a place to learn to be better, and not necessarily to fix anything that's wrong.

"So, it seems like you're not quite sure about what you want here," says the therapist.

The client starts to wonder if they're wasting this professional's time.

"No, not exactly. It's just...I'm sorry, I don't know how this goes. I suppose you see a lot of people every day with *real* problems..."

"You don't think your problems are real, then?"

"Um. Hmm. That's not what I meant. It's not that I have...problems, it's more like, I just want to be the best version of myself, you know?"

"It's OK. There's nothing to be ashamed about. Seeking help for your problems doesn't mean you're weak, you know."

The rest of the session carries on but the client has already decided, in this first two minutes, never to return to therapy again. Why? For those who are skilled listeners, the reason is probably obvious: the therapist did a *really* bad job of listening. Did you catch it? Let's review.

Firstly, the therapist *tells* the client what they feel, without checking whether their interpretation is correct, or even wanted. It's a series of statements and assumptions rather than acceptance. The therapist had their own version of events and conclusions likely before the patient even sat down.

How frustrating. Rather than figuring out what exactly the client is experiencing, the therapist has some preconceived mold they're forcing onto the conversation, completely ignoring what the client actually wants from them.

Sadly, this state of miscommunication and poor listening is more common than it first seems, and many people—perhaps like our therapist—will never even know the extent to which their listening techniques are just not working for them and those they're speaking with. This is a book about a skill that may be *simple*, but is certainly not *easy*. Listening is at the heart of proper communication, which itself is at the heart of every meaningful connection you can have with another human being. In other words, learning to listen matters! If even trained therapists (whose true focus should be to listen and absorb and then provide feedback) can't always hit the mark, then what chance do we stand? Well, as always, learning and gaining the necessary skills is the first step, and that's what this book provides.

Not being a deep listener doesn't mean you're a bad person. Gaining self-awareness and understanding the "meta conversation" are skills like any other—meaning they can be learnt and improved upon, whoever you are. In fact, lacking these skills means you're quite normal, as the instinct we are all born with is to be somewhat self-centered. And yet, some of us are naturally good listeners, but most people need a little deliberate effort to get there. Some of us are only good *at* listening, and are terrible at telling stories to others or even expressing emotions. However, unlike the way some of us are born taller, shorter, or with black or brown hair, listening is a quality that you have complete control over—starting now.

Being a good listener is not some grand charitable gesture, or a thing you do purely for the sake of other people. When we actually engage with attention and thoughtfulness with another person's world, *everyone* benefits, and we only enrich our own perspective. It's the quintessential win-win—even more than you might imagine. At least, that's the first important mindset shift you must make to be a better listener.

The True Win-Win

A large piece of the puzzle in creating a presence optimized for listening is the age-old piece of advice, popularized by Dale

Carnegie and his famous book *How to Win Friends and Influence People.*

Much of his advice is now derided as common sense, even though the very reason it's deemed so obvious is because of *his* book. Perhaps one of his best pieces of advice was simply to get people to talk, or even brag, about themselves. He was quoted, "You can make more friends in two months by becoming interested in other people than you can in two years by trying to get other people interested in you."

It turns out that Carnegie was correct, right down to the biological level. A 2012 study conducted by neuroscientists Diana Tamir and Jason Mitchell at Harvard University entitled "Disclosing Information About the Self Is Intrinsically Rewarding" found that our urge to share personal information with others is one of the most fundamental and powerful parts of being human.

Brain images showed that sharing information about ourselves triggers the same sensations in our brains that we experience when we eat food and have sex—two behaviors that we are biologically compelled to do. Thus, it seems we are biologically compelled to share and communicate our thoughts.

One method the researchers used to determine how much the participants valued being able to talk about themselves was to offer a modest financial incentive to anybody who would answer questions about *other* people instead. Some of the questions involved casual subjects such as hobbies and personal tastes while others covered personality traits, such as intelligence, curiosity, or aggression.

The researchers found that many of the participants were willing to pass up on the money, preferring the rewarding feelings of self-disclosure over financial gain. In fact, the average participant gave up between 17 and 25 percent of their possible earnings just so that they could reveal personal information.

Researchers then used a functional magnetic resonance imaging scanner (fMRI) to observe what parts of the brain were most excited when the subjects were talking about themselves. Again, they found a correlation between self-disclosure and heightened activity in brain regions belonging to the mesolimbic dopamine system—the same region that's associated with the satisfying feeling we get from food, money, and sex. This increased brain activity even happens when we speak about ourselves *without* anyone listening to us. Of course, there is a far more powerful effect when our listening skills come into play.

Unconscious Obstacles

If there's so much value in being a good listener, why are so few people actually good at it? Instead of thinking in terms of skills or attributes you lack, think instead of the barriers that keep you from truly listening to another person. All the skills and techniques in the world won't help if we still retain false beliefs, habits and blind spots that get in the way of real connection and empathy. It would be like owning a boat and being an expert seaman, but having a deathly fear of the water. Some things just overshadow others.

Let's take a closer look at what some of these barriers might be.

Think about the poor listeners you may have encountered in your own life. What made you feel they weren't listening to you? Perhaps the biggest problem may be their ***inability to look outside of themselves and their own needs***. This doesn't mean that they have real or actual needs, it simply means that they are focused only on themselves and their reality.

Good conversation is like a tennis match where the attention moves equally between the two parties, like a tennis ball. If someone is never able to truly put their attention on anything other than themselves, it's like playing tennis with a person who never properly serves the ball, or never returns it once it goes over the net. A conversation suddenly turns into a monologue, soliloquy, or simply a lecture to an unwilling student.

So-called "conversational narcissism" may look on its surface like a regular conversation, but on closer inspection it actually resembles two people spouting monologues in close proximity to one another! In a way, good conversation is a dying art precisely because people feel more isolated than ever before.

With so many people missing the feeling of being truly heard themselves, they crave attention and to be in the spotlight, having others listen closely to them. The sad irony is that such a person can bring a selfish, even competitive attitude to an activity that is supposed to be mutually beneficial. And thus the cycle continues and grows even worse over time, spurred on by feelings of not being heard or paid attention to. Using a conversation as a platform to win attention and stroke your ego is undoubtedly a losing strategy.

Have you ever quietly waited for someone to stop speaking, thinking all the while about what you would say the moment they shut up? If so, you've likely been guilty of conversational narcissism too! It is still the inability to put aside your own internal monologue completely, and focus on what the other person is thinking or saying. Same end outcome of dueling monologues.

So to start with, improve your listening skills by being vigilant about the ways in which craving attention can make you a worse conversationalist. The idea is not to always seek to turn attention to yourself. Conversations should be thought of not as a means to win attention, but to *share* it enjoyably with someone else. The goal is not competition for the floor, but cooperation with an ally. The purpose is to collaborate, not express solely. The aim is to learn, not teach, and so on. For some of us, this may require a complete re-tooling of what we seek when we want to be social.

After an ineffective conversation, people may feel depleted, bored, or even more alone. Good conversations, on the other hand, can be things of beauty, allowing both participants to create between them something bigger than the sum of its parts. And remember how much people were willing to pay to be heard and express themselves in the study referenced earlier in this very chapter?

Listening well requires that you suspend your own self-interest and ego and gracefully allow someone else to shine.

It's now time to get self-conscious and introspective. Sociologist Charles Derber has studied this phenomenon extensively and believes that this form of conversational narcissism can occur without people even being aware it's going on. It can be easy to imagine that conversational narcissists are the stereotypical loudmouths who dominate conversation—but it's far subtler than this. It turns out that the situation can turn on a single word choice. He articulated what he called *support responses* and *shift responses*, and how they can subtly pervade our everyday vocabulary.

Derber explains what he calls "initiatives" in conversation—which can be *attention giving* or *attention seeking*, the latter of which can be further divided into active or passive. For our purposes, you can guess which of the two we want to orient toward.

Let's look at some examples of both in conversation.

For the active, attention-giving variety, a "*support response*" maintains attention on the speaker and their topic—for example, asking a question about what's been said. Support responses can be simple acknowledgements ("Oh really?" "Uh huh"), positively supporting ("that's great!"), or in question form ("What did you say then?"). For instance:

"I love French films."
"Which is your favorite?"

The "*shift response,*" however, is an active attention-seeking response that shifts the attention to the other person, in other words back to themselves. It's an act of grabbing the spotlight and pointing it in the opposite direction.

"I love French films."
"Yeah? I've never cared much about movies. The other day, actually, I saw this thing at the cinema…"

This isn't to say that shift responses are always wrong—in context, they can work, especially if the other person subtly reclaims attention again. Sometimes it might even behoove you to use more shift responses to grab some of the spotlight, or make your feelings known. But how much are you using them?

If you have two people with poor listening skills, and both are hell-bent on shift responses, you end up with a wrestling match for attention, rather than a conversation. Maybe both parties are satisfying their lust for expression, but their gas tanks for being heard are running on empty. You may not notice if you are locked in this type of battle, but from the outside looking in, observing this kind of interaction can be curious and confusing.

Moreover, if a bad conversationalist (someone who continually uses shift responses) is paired with a very empathetic listener (someone who continually uses support responses), one party may well feel as though they're having a good talk because the other person is consistently offering support responses, while the other wants to jump off a bridge because the conversation is turning into an awkward pseudo-lecture on the other person's life and beliefs.

What about passive conversational narcissism? Naturally, some people are still quite aware of social norms and etiquette and so will vie for attention in subtler ways. One way of doing this is to fail to offer support responses, waiting till the other person's thread dies away and you can take the limelight. Here, you are hoping that the other person runs out of steam so you can finally get your word in. It is like sitting in a tree and waiting for the prey to get tired and go to sleep—you know it will happen eventually, so you passively bide your time.

Have you been part of a conversation where the other person didn't offer any support responses, even a quaint "Oh really?" or "Uh-huh"? You're not quite sure whether they've taken in what you've said, and that may be intentional on their part. It may have been a case of passive conversational narcissism.

Most of us are taught that it's polite to not ramble on, to take your turn and then rest, and to share space in conversations. Fine, this person will follow those basic rules. But they sure won't encourage their conversation partner to speak more, lest it cut into their own speaking time! A lack of (genuine!) feedback from the other person can quickly make someone feel they ought to stop speaking—and this is where the conversational narcissist steps back into the picture.

Though it's tempting to try to catch other people in the act of conversational narcissism, its far more productive to learn to notice it in yourself and guard against it. You can't control what others do, but you can control your actions and how good of a listener you are. After all, that is the goal of this book. For the other purpose, you may want to seek a book on persuasion or hypnosis.

The irony is it's often those who are able to listen well, to step aside, and to take a genuine interest in their conversation partners who become people we think of as most interesting, charismatic and worthy of our attention in the first place. So the purported goal of conversational narcissism (*making darn sure that people know things about you*) isn't even satisfied. Oops. Luckily, there are a few guidelines to battle these unconscious obstacles you'll undoubtedly face.

Balance your needs and desires with other people's

To do this, you first need to be aware of your focus and where it's going. Pay attention to how the airtime is being distributed. Is one person doing all the talking? Is there a back-and-forth? This requires more than just playing at being interested in another person's life—you genuinely need to forget yourself for a moment and engage fully, and honestly, in what someone else is saying. Stop thinking about your response for the future, and pay attention to what someone is currently saying to you.

This means no rushing in to explain or frame what they've said so that it relates back to you again. Give more supportive responses, and guard against constantly referring every topic back to yourself. Ask questions to invite the other person to say more. If you take attention for a while, enjoy it—but volley it back again. Like we were taught as children: It's good to share!

"As you were talking, it made me think about this experience I had once, where XYZ. That made me wonder, did you find that XYZ was the case as well?" A person saying this demonstrates that they're willing to share the conversation, rather than hog it all for themselves.

Think about ego, power, self-esteem and control

Those who seem most boastful in a conversation, who jealously guard attention or speak over others, are often those who feel most insecure in themselves. Their need to control the conversation comes from a hunger for attention and approval. If you find yourself using conversations as a platform to boost your ego, feel better about yourself or be witnessed and supported by others, your work may be to learn to be comfortable taking the back seat for a change. The paradox is that people who seem most likeable and confident are those who don't appear to be making frantic efforts to dominate others' attention.

Be egalitarian

Do you have any unconscious beliefs about what conversations are actually for? Some people speak because they want a soapbox to share their opinions, or they want to "teach" others and tell them exactly what's what, or simply to demonstrate superiority in some way or another. Become aware of *why* you're conversing. Are you genuinely curious about the human being in front of you? Have you already made up your mind about them, or do you simply see them as an audience for your agenda (which you refuse to stray from), a sparring partner, a competitor?

Good listeners stay in the moment, and don't get distracted with their own concerns when they're meant to be focused on someone else. Try to treat conversations as pleasurable opportunities to give and take, and to witness another as much as revealing oneself.

Does it frequently end up being the case that your conversation partners know a ton about you, but you don't know very much about them? This would mean that the flow of information is decidedly one-sided, and that you are monopolizing the air space. Do you actually ask others questions? When is the last time you asked five questions in a row?

All of this leads us round again to the most important conversation skill—listening. Great communicators tend to speak *less* than poor communicators. Though the ego might not like it, the truth is that you don't become a good conversationalist by telling the best jokes or stories, by being the most interesting or impressive, or by speaking the most. You do it by being humble, friendly, and intrigued by how interesting *other people* are. *The secret is to be more interested than interesting.* Learn, rather than teach. Listen, rather than speak. Allow others to express, knowing there's enough to go around. Connect rather than impress. Share or participate in a story, rather than merely telling it.

But They're Boring...

No, you are.

You may have read through the previous sections and wondered how realistic it is to be completely enthralled with what another person is saying. It can certainly make people feel good to be the center of your attention, but what if you literally don't feel it? It's not a great thing to admit, but many of us secretly think that other people simply aren't that interesting, and it's hard to care about what they have to say. It's tempting to look at the work it takes to listen to someone's seemingly mundane story and decide you'd rather not bother.

We can sometimes miss the point. Sometimes, it's a question of unrealistic expectations. A conversation doesn't necessarily have to blow your socks off or be massively useful to you to be worth taking part in. And of course it's normal to not be interested in literally everyone you meet—some people will spark curiosity, others less so. Finally, it's not necessary at all to fake it, or act in ways that drain and bore you. Frankly, it is possible to be a warm and friendly person with a good social life who doesn't launch into ecstatic conversation with everyone they encounter.

But here's where socially successful people have a subtler understanding than those who love calling themselves introverts or feel like other people are boring and not worth their time.

Have a little faith, suspend judgment and—again—just listen. Drop any preconceived ideas about what makes a person interesting—some of the most fascinating people are out there, just a few pointed questions away from being discovered. Be open to being proven wrong, to being surprised. Decide to actively look for the good and the interesting in others. It's an old adage that "you can learn something from everyone," and it's true. Look at conversation as a means of finding out exactly what that thing is.

If you immediately judge someone as uninteresting, they will undoubtedly remain that for you. Judge them differently, and they will become that as well. Use this to your advantage.

It's rude to assume people are boring simply because they don't wow you after a few minutes, especially when you may be assisting in it by lobbing boring questions at them. This in itself can be rather narcissistic—to think of other people in terms of their entertainment value to you, rather than as individuals in their own right. When you don't really know someone, it's hard to be concerned about the mundane details of their lives, but you'd certainly care more if they were very important people to you.

The idea is that people are not boring, exactly, but just that you don't know them well enough to care. You can see the catch-22—you can only get to know someone if you first go through the "boring" small talk and try to forge a closer connection. Being sociable is something that builds on itself. It starts with extending a gesture of goodwill to the other person. You don't know that they're interesting, but you hope and expect they are, and you reach out in faith that your investment will be worth it later on.

In other words, some people enter conversations expecting an immediate payoff, whereas in reality it's more common that you need to invest a little first, and wait patiently for a reward that may take a while.

You don't need to force anything. Just be open and receptive and give it a go—at least for a while. Even if you never uncover something of interest in talking to another person, you can still do so with compassion and politeness, and you may just learn something about yourself in the process— how to be a better conversationalist, for one. Some people will take more than one conversation to open up. Do your part by building trust and rapport, asking questions and listening.

You may be surprised what happens if you have the expectation that you will find something delightful or fascinating. People can have unexpected hobbies or completely out-there experiences, skills, values, and so on that may be of interest to you even though some other parts of their life aren't. Don't be afraid to push a little and ask questions that invite more intimacy.

Go beyond the surface and ask how your conversation partner feels about certain things. You can always divulge a little about yourself first to put them at ease. Along this vein, you might need to "go first" sometimes when opening up with people. Give unexpected answers, be truthful and make an effort at being honest and genuine. People are often more than willing to respond in kind.

If you're *still* not convinced that anyone has anything interesting to tell you, it may legitimately be a case of not hanging around with the right kinds of people. You may need to seek conversations with those you have more in common with than coworkers, fellow students or even family members—

who might be easily available conversation partners, but won't necessarily be your "people."

Sometimes, broadening yourself and the range of things that interest you has the effect of making other people seem more interesting. Dabble, take risks, and avoid assuming you know what things are before you try them. Failing to properly listen to others could be part of a broader discomfort around other people, feelings of low self-worth, depression, anxiety or an unhappiness in your own life.

People who have been bullied or mistreated by others can take a haughty, condescending tone as a defense mechanism, or a way to cover up the fact that they feel it's *others* who don't like *them*. As we've already seen, having the perspective that others are enemies or rivals can kill a social life.

Finally, feeling disinterested in others can simply be a phase of life, a period of immaturity or a result of being a certain age or living in a certain environment. Younger people can often consider something worthless unless they can personally get something out of it—it takes experience and wisdom to move away from this self-interest and toward healthy relationships with others.

All Hail Conan

I've found that the absolute best mindset to emulate for deep listening is that of a talk-show host—Jimmy Fallon, Jimmy Kimmel, Conan O'Brien, whoever your favorite is, they all do the same thing. Just ask yourself what they would do if you're struggling for what curiosity looks like and how you can wield it. Conan O'Brien happens to be my favorite, so let's think about the traits he embodies in a conversation with a guest on his show.

Visualize his studio. He's got a big open space, and he is seated at a desk. His guest is seated at a chair adjacent to the desk, and it's literally like they exist in a world of their own. When Conan has a guest on his show, that guest is the center of his world for the next ten minutes. They are the most interesting person he has ever come across, everything they say is spellbinding, he is insatiably curious about their stories, and he reacts to anything they say with an uproarious laugh and an otherwise exaggerated reaction that they were seeking. He is charmingly positive and can always find a humorous spin on a negative aspect of a story.

His sole purpose is to make his guest comfortable on the show, encourage them to talk about themselves, and ultimately make them feel good and look good. In turn, this makes them share things they might not otherwise reveal and creates a connection and chemistry that is so important for a talk show. The viewers at home are desperate to learn about this celebrity guest, so Conan acts as a proxy for their curiosity. Also, the viewers can tell in an instant if either party is mailing it in or faking it, so Conan's job literally depends on his ability to use his curiosity to connect on a deeper level.

Even with grumpy or more quiet guests, he is able to elevate their energy levels and attitudes simply by being intensely interested in them (at an energy level slightly above theirs) and encouraging them by giving the great reactions they seek. It's almost as if he plays the game "How little can I say to get the most out of people?"

Of course, in your life, this applies to those people you come across that are like pulling teeth to talk to. A little bit of friendly encouragement and affirmation can make even the meekest clam open up. Numerous questions, directing the conversation toward them, and the feeling that you actually care are also integral. Imagine the relief you can create at dreaded networking events. People like those who like them, so when you react the way they want, it encourages them to be more outgoing and open with you.

Another talk-show host would later go on the record lamenting how often he disliked his guests and how boring he found the actors and actresses that he would be forced to speak to. But that's a testament to how highly trained his habit of curiosity was. He started by making a conscious decision to be curious, built the habit, and engaged his guests easily; do you think his guests could tell if he was truly interested or not? Never.

Curiosity allows people to feel comfortable enough to speak freely beyond a superficial level—because you are demonstrating that you care and that you will listen when they open up. People won't be inclined to reveal their secret thoughts if they think they'll be met with apathy, after all. So even if you have to fake it till you make it, Conan O'Brien is who your mindset and attitude should feel like.

In case Conan O'Brien's curiosity still isn't coming naturally to you, here are some more specific patterns of thought you can use to improve your people skills.

I wonder what they are like? When you start to wonder about the other person, it changes your perspective on them completely. This is an inkling of curiosity. You start to care about them—not only about their shallow traits, such as their occupation or how their day is going, but what motivates them and makes them act in the way they do.

Having a sense of wonder about someone is one of the most powerful mindsets you can possess because it makes you want to scratch your itch. Scratching the itch of curiosity will become secondary to everything else because you simply want to know about the other person.

Suppose you had a sense of wonder about computers as a child. You probably irritated others with how many questions you asked anyone that seemed to have knowledge about computers. Now as an adult, what kind of attention span are you going to devote to computers, and what kind of questions are you going to ask? You are going to skip the small-talk interview questions and get right down to the details because it's what you care and are curious about.

Keeping the mindset of wonderment will completely change the way you interact with people because you will suddenly care, and much of the time, we don't notice that we don't care about the person we are talking to. You'll dig deeper and deeper until you can put together a picture of what you are wondering about.

What can they teach me? Don't read this from the perspective of attempting to gain what you can from someone. Instead see others as being people worthy of your attention. Everyone has valuable knowledge, whether it applies to your life or not. Everyone is great at something, and everyone is a domain expert in something that you are not, no matter how small or obscure the subject.

The main point is to ignite an interest in the other person as opposed to an apathetic approach. Imagine if you were a huge skiing junkie and you met someone who used to be a professional skier. They may have even reached the Olympics in their prime.

What will follow? You'll be thrilled by what you can potentially learn and gain from the other person, and that will guide the entire interaction. Again, there will be a level of interest and engagement if you view others as worthy of talking to. But you'll never know unless you dig below the surface.

Whether we like to admit it or not, sometimes we feel some people are not worth our time. It's a bad habit, and this line of thinking is one of the first steps toward breaking it. Everyone is worth our time, but we won't be able to discover it if we don't put in the work.

What do we have in common? This is an investigation into the life experiences you share with someone. It instantly makes them more engaging and interesting— because we feel that they are more similar to us! It may sound a bit egotistical, but we are undoubtedly more captivated by people who share our same views and interests.

Finding commonalities may even *elevate* people, especially if we are surrounded by people different from us. For instance, if you discovered that a new stranger was born in the same hospital as you were, despite being in a different country, you would instantly feel more open to them. This person *must* share similar worldviews, values, and humor. But you wouldn't have discovered that if you didn't make an attempt at excavating beneath the surface.

You will need to go on a hunt, and you will ask the important questions that get you where you want to be. You might jump from topic to topic, or you might dive in and ask directly.

Perhaps it's just because you will have something to fixate on besides talking for talking's sake, but these attitudes will drastically change how you approach people. Curiosity can still be tough to maintain, which is why my final suggestion for creating curiosity is to make a game of it. Your goal is to learn as much about the other person as possible. Alternatively, assume there is something extremely thrilling and exciting about the other person and make it your quest to uncover it. Eventually, you'll find what you're looking for.

The next time you go out to a café or store, put these attitudes to the test with the captive audience of the baristas or cashiers you come across—the lucky few who are paid to be nice to you. Do you perceive these workers to be below you, or do you treat them differently than you would a good friend? Do you have a sense of wonderment and curiosity about them? What do you think they can teach you, and what do you have in common with them?

Do you tend to ask the baristas or cashiers about their day and actually care about their answer? If not, do you think you'll be able to simply "turn it on" when you're around people you care about? Practice changing your mindsets concerning the people around you. It's the easiest practice you'll have because you don't have to lift a finger, but it drastically transforms the quality of relationships you'll create.

Takeaways:

- We've all got two ears but only one mouth, right? This means we should do about double the listening versus speaking, but the truth is doing so goes against our natural instinct. We are wired to express and talk about ourselves—to the extent that it provides the same type of neurological stimulation as sex. Fair enough, but that doesn't mean talking nonstop is acceptable or helpful to our relationships.

- It's time to view listening as the true win-win in cultivating deeper relationships. When you listen, you not only get to learn about someone, you are (paradoxically to some) seen as more charismatic, interesting, and enjoyable to interact with. So if your end goal is to be those things, listening is the skill you must perfect. It's a simple skill, but certainly nothing close to easy.

- The challenge is that there are so many unconscious ways we wrest control over a conversation and become a conversational narcissist. This is simply when someone speaks so much that it appears to be a monologue versus a shared dialogue. One subtle way this occurs is through support versus shift responses, where the feeling you impart to others can hinge on a single vocabulary choice. The underlying theme, however, is to accept letting go of control, pride, and ego, and go wherever someone else wishes to go.

- A more conscious obstacle many people face is the feeling that the people they interact with are quite boring and have nothing worthwhile to say; thus, listening to them is not a good use of their time. Just reading that sentence, you should be able to spot a few flaws. If you think most people you run across are boring, you're the boring one. You're letting a prejudgment dictate your actions, and ruin your interactions. Instead, expect that you will find something fascinating and delightful, and that's just what will begin to happen.

- For a role model on how to draw information out of people, look no further than late-night talk-show hosts. Their sole job is to make a celebrity, often no funnier than you or I, appear immensely charming and intelligent. That's a tough task sometimes. Think about the energy, focus, attention, and listening they employ to make this happen. That's what is possible.

Chapter 2. Styles, Frames, and Levels

Picture a scene that may feel all too familiar to some couples. Person X has had a bad experience and is upset, and is now telling person Y about what happened. Person Y is listening—truly listening—and yet the conversation isn't going well and eventually ends poorly. It goes like this:

X: I had such an awful time at work today. Ugh, I hate my job.
Y: Oh? I thought you liked it there. What's the problem?

X: I don't know, I just sometimes feel like I never get a break, like I'm rushed off my feet the second I walk in the door…

Y: Really? I'm sure you said you were enjoying the work last week.

X: Well, yes, I mean of course I enjoy it sometimes. I just feel so unappreciated, you know?
Y: Uh-huh. Maybe you should ask for a raise.

X: No, it's not that. Today Z didn't even bother to thank me for basically baling him out of an emergency, and I felt so…
Y: Have you told Z? Anyway, you are Z's superior, so…

X: I *know* that. But does that mean I just have to carry everyone's slack, forever?
Y: So… you didn't tell Z how you feel?

X: You're not listening! It's not about Z!
Y: Yeesh, then what *is* it about? I keep asking but you're not telling me anything.
X: Ugh, just forget it.

What's gone wrong here? Y may genuinely be interested in continuing the conversation, wanting to "help" and doing all the things we've discussed as good conversational technique. But Y still doesn't feel listened to—and it's because they have different listening styles, and are seemingly unaware of the fact. It's more or less as simple as someone being right or left-handed—there's a natural instinct and course of action, but that doesn't mean that it can or should work optimally. As a result of our backgrounds, experiences, and preferences, we all have certain approaches to the world. So should it be surprising when our approach doesn't line up with someone else's, creating a type of listening nightmare?

We've taken a look at some of the skills and attitudes we can develop to make us better listeners and, in turn, better communicators and more effective and balanced people. This chapter is again going to consider just how important it is to be aware of the strengths and weaknesses in your own communication style, before you attempt to learn any new techniques or skills.

A way to understand the conversation above is to acknowledge that even when people are listening, they may have different *ways* of listening—and clashing styles can often lead to misunderstandings or conflict. As with so much in social mastery, it comes down to awareness, and the willingness to be flexible enough to prioritize connecting with those around us.

People, Emotion, and Heart

Psychologist Larry Barker proposed four different communication styles, based on people's preferences, personalities and the purpose of their conversation with you. When we consider the conversation that started out the chapter, we can plainly see that we must understand and tailor our communication style to that of other people in order to listen more effectively.

Barker's first approach is the "**people-oriented**" style, which, as it sounds, is a listening style that pays attention to people as a whole and their feelings. These are cooperative, collective-minded people who try to understand others, have empathy, and develop cohesion and harmony in a group. While going too far in this can be a problem (i.e. being a bit irrational, getting carried away with emotion, violating boundaries or getting overwhelmed), for the most part this is a great style to adopt if your goal is to connect interpersonally, and improve relationships of all kinds.

In our example, X was communicating an *emotional* story—it involved their feelings about an event, and they were seeking empathy, understanding and a witness for these emotions.

However, Y was not people oriented, but what's called "**content-oriented**" in their listening style. When these people listen, they are homing in on facts, data and *what* is said, rather than how it is said or who is saying it. They may seek to confirm the credibility of the speaker rather than offer support and compassion—after all, in their mind, the purpose of the conversation may be to find facts or solve problems.

Such a listening style is more hands-off, neutral and impersonal, but probes for details, looking for patterns or cause and effect, trying to unpack the logical argument in a story rather than the human content. Understandably, an approach like this can be disastrous if used excessively in more intimate contexts, and is more suited for business or formal relationships.

As you might have guessed, Y in our example was listening to X's story, but "hearing" only the literal facts. Instead of understanding what was needed or the spirit in which the conversation was instigated, Y instead tried to ascertain whether what X said was true ("But didn't you say...") or suggest solutions to a problem that X wasn't really presenting as the conflict ("You should ask for a pay raise").

Though there is no bad intent, the conversation ends poorly primarily because Y fails to see that their listening style isn't appropriate to the situation, and responds on the wrong level. The reverse could also be true: if X and Z from work were to discuss the issue, they would both fare better by adopting a more content-focused approach.

There are two other styles in Barker's theory, however, and some natural overlap between each. "**Action-oriented**" listeners are curious about what needs to be done or has been done already, who does it, and what actions are underway. For them, things need to be clear, obvious and translatable to the real world. When mismatched in style, these listeners can appear impatient, controlling or dismissive of others, responding to thoughts or emotions with a sort of "so what?" attitude. Leaders and those in action-focused careers may find themselves stuck in this approach to the detriment of their personal relationships.

Finally, possibly "**time-oriented**" listeners put most of their attention on time and how it plays out in stories, requests or conversations. They are typically focused on schedules, and keeping conversations trimmed into neat time blocks they can manage predictably. In listening to others, they will constantly be seeking to "wrap up," summarize, get to the point, or refer back to time in some way. For those in other groups, this can feel like a strange focus, resulting in both parties feeling annoyed and sidetracked.

The key thing here is that none of these tendencies are fixed—we can all move from one style to another, but it may take some effort and practice, especially for those who are quite attached to their styles. No style is better or worse than the other; rather, an effective communicator is someone who is aware of each approach as tools in an inventory that they can switch out as needed. The important thing is to maintain awareness of your own context, and the needs of both yourself and others, to pick an approach that has the best chance of success for everyone involved.

These different listening styles can be framed a slightly different way according to the theories of educational psychologist Benjamin Bloom, although versions of this theory are perhaps thousands of years old. People can be understood as having a general preference for **feeling** (the heart, emotional), **thinking** (the head, cognitive), or **doing** (the hands, behavioral).

Those with a preference for approaching life with their heads (thinking) are like the "content-oriented" people above, and will likely frame problems as a matter of lack of knowledge or insufficient understanding. When you talk to such a person, it's helpful to acknowledge that they learn new things and engage with their world via rational, structured, cognitive means.

This could result in the preference for more goal-oriented "informational listening"— active listening for facts, details, arguments or data in much the same way as a student might listen intently to a lecture. While this is great for corporate environments or in universities, it's less ideal in romantic relationships, as our previous example with X and Y shows.

Similarly, this orientation may favor a more critical kind of listening, wherein information is analyzed and appraised for its veracity, coherence and value. Importantly, this is still rather content-focused, especially if such a listener has neglected to consider the emotions and desires of the speaker as relevant data. Such people may look down on action-oriented speakers and find them unintelligent, or secretly prefer clean and abstract theory to the messy real world. They may similarly fear emotions and have a strong need to control others' feelings when they encounter them.

An example is a doctor who listens intently to a patient's story but only filters out the medical facts in order to make a diagnosis, while ignoring emotional content. A lawyer may listen to a client or colleague speaking about a case and actively try to hear out missing information, flaws in an argument, opportunities, and weaknesses. The goal is to listen for some very specific purpose—to gather as much good-quality data as possible in order to do the job properly.

"Hands" people act first and think later, or, more accurately, they seem to think *by* doing. To them, direct, real-world experience is the gold standard, and they engage with the world via their psychomotor skills, and working through the hands. Sensible and practical, they may have a reciprocal disdain for overly cognitive thinker types, believing these people waste time and lack real-world understanding of problems. Similarly, they may get irritated with "soft," heart-centered or emotion and relationship-focused people, feeling that they lack will or a backbone.

An example is a manager at work who is listening to an employee's account of a problem in the office. Even though the employee may be relaying plenty of neutral information, along with some emotional details ("everyone in sales is sweating bullets now…"), the manager might only listen for what he feels is crucial information: what has the employee actually done so far, and did it work? He might not care much for theories, rumination, worry or analysis. For him, not much matters until it's been put into action.

"Heart" people prioritize emotional, relational and holistic content first, and engage with the world through their own felt direct experience, as well as striving for harmony and connectedness. What matters to heart people are motivations, values, appreciation, feelings and relationships. They may practice appreciative or empathetic listening—wherein the goal is merely to show support or sympathy, and encourage the speaker. Often, this is the true reaction we want in others, and it's the type of interaction that fosters deeper relationships and open dialogue. It's a large part of the type of listening we want to train in this book, though the others are of course not without their purposes and benefits.

An example of a heart approach is someone who is able to hear a friend talk and simply listen attentively, perhaps occasionally asking a question or offering a supportive sound or phrase. The stereotypical "how does that make you feel?" is broadly considered poor practice, but all good psychologists, counselors, carers, and so on are in effect adopting this position in their conversation—they want to know what the other person is feeling, and the details are somewhat secondary.

People listening from a heart perspective are able to access a valuable interpersonal skill. Though not all heart-oriented people will necessarily be empathetic or excellent listeners, it's fair to say that one cannot connect on a deeply personal and human level without being in the heart.

Empathetic listening is listening without judgment, interruption or a need to fix the other person, and with the intent to simply hear and understand another person's experience as it is. Ideally, the therapist we encountered in the beginning of this book would use empathetic listening, rather than assuming that he already knew exactly what his client was saying. Heart-focused people may find the emphasis on the intellect to be cold and even inhuman, and feel wary of those who neglect their own or other people's emotions.

Of course, all of this categorizing people into different groups is arguably a "head" activity and not meant to offer definitive rules about humans so much as suggest patterns that could help us all deal with one another more effectively. For our purposes, those who are comfortable with and proficient in the "heart" skills are invariably good communicators. While we have the goal of being aware of, accommodating or switching to different modes as needed, we might need to begin with the affective and emotional perspective.

The Correct Frame

Closely related to this discussion of listening styles and unique conversational perspectives is the idea of "frames." In reading the previous few paragraphs you might have correctly noticed that the kinds of listening people use also has a lot to do with context. It matters who you're speaking to, why, and what the preceding situation was. What is someone looking for, what is your natural style, and how do you have to reframe things to communicate better? These are questions you should at least have a passing relationship with.

Our earlier example between X and Y could be less about their individual personalities and listening styles and more to do with the fact that they were simply not sharing a conversational frame—one wanted sympathy while the other was trying to offer advice and practical suggestions.

In a way, *frame differences* can explain much of interpersonal conflict, and if you can become adept at noticing them, you may give yourself a powerful tool to resolving misunderstandings.

So, what's a frame? A frame is like a point of view, but instead of concerning one person, it's more like a temporary platform that two or more people occupy when they share a conversation.

Your frame may be about asserting a power dynamic, solving a problem, mutually validating one another, exchanging information, complaining, talking casually for its own sake, picking apart a misunderstanding, sharing guidance or wisdom, and so on. A frame is the background, the unspoken goal of the conversation. Properly understanding how frames shape interpersonal interactions can give you a deeper insight into being a better listener and conversationalist.

Though it's possible to have conflict with a shared frame (for example, two people can share the frame of fighting or competing), matched or aligned frames usually lead to better understanding all round, while mismatched frames can cause complete communication breakdown.

For example:

- a woman is trying to get help from a shop assistant, but the employee is more interested in flirting with her;
- someone phones a call center technical helpline not realizing that the person on the other end of the line is not there to share personal grievances about the company or product;
- a friend is relaxing on the weekend and wants to enjoy some pleasant, idle chitchat, but his friend wants to get embroiled in a deep, gut-wrenching philosophical conversation;
- someone offers up a playful joke but a person overhears and decides to "correct" them, completely missing the intention and tone in which the joke was made...
- someone vents about their supervisor at work and wants to let off steam, but the

listener instantly draws up a to-do list to passive-aggressively make the supervisor's life terrible.

You get the idea.

For many of us, playing with frames and understanding what each unique situation requires will lead to the following: embracing the fact that a solution is not being sought, and again, simple listening and imparting the feeling of being heard is the priority of the day.

A mismatched frame is a difference in conversational goals—and this difference means that neither party actually gets their needs or goals met. It's possible that *one* party is satisfied, but typically only a matched frame gets both people what they want quickly.

If there's a mismatch, the most important first step is to notice it. You'll know something is off if a conversation feels awkward, stilted or frustrating—or if you can sense the other person is feeling these things (this is where heart focus comes in handy!). Mismatched frame conversations can often feel like they're going round in circles, or getting more confusing rather than less so, or are simply boring.

Next, try to see if you can loosely identify your own and the other person's conversational goals. Mismatch ends when you both get on the same page—they adopt your frame, you adopt theirs, or you both adopt a new shared one. It's also possible to agree to work within different frames, as long as you acknowledge shared goals. It can help to refer to an external authority or yardstick to guide your interactions ("you say X and I say Y, but let's just consult the handbook and agree to do what it says").

What do you do, though, if the other person's conversational goal is "to hold these people as a hostage audience while I regale them with tales about how utterly awesome I am," and your goal is just to have a nice time at your friend's party? Conversational narcissists, bullies, angry people or those with an axe to grind or a niggle they want to complain about may not *want* to change frames—and when dealing with them, you might not want to either.

Here, it's wise to acknowledge that not all conversations are viable, and sometimes the best course for an interaction to take is for it to terminate, or at best be postponed. Call out a bad frame if you see it and think it will help, but if someone is hell-bent on engaging you from a destructive or nonsensical perspective, you can always choose to opt out.

Learning mastery in working with frames will not only help you navigate social situations in real time, but will offer you a broader overall picture of your communication style in general. What frame do you usually adopt and why? Is it working for your general goals in life? If you fail to properly communicate at times, why is that and what can you do next time to be better? You can also read and analyze people more effectively if you simply think about their probable frames.

Amazing listeners have taken an active, hands-on approach to their engagements with others, rather than just behaving unconsciously out of habit, never considering the effectiveness of their tools. You don't need to do anything more complicated than regularly check that you're on the same page as others, and guard against getting stuck in just one frame or listening style.

What does someone want out of this interaction/event/conversation/chat/venting session? It may not seem difficult, but this simple step is foreign in practice. Does asking this question sound laborious? It can be, but it's really just about taking yourself out of the equation and considering what someone else wants first and foremost. Putting yourself first is a habit that is deeply ingrained and hard to break.

Five Levels of Listening

As we continue our journey through different types of styles and frames, we end this chapter with a section on different levels of listening, and what is generally more effective for becoming a deep listener. *Unlike* previously, there is no particular use for some of these levels of listening, and they just demonstrate a shifting amount of focus and attentional generosity.

There are five different levels of listening that we experience, from total ignorance to almost consuming attention. Most of our lives we sort of float through the first four levels, which all reflect at least a measure of self-interest. In other words, in those four levels we still use our own reference points to interpret what the other person is saying (if we're listening at all). Many of us can hope to get to level four at best, and even that stage we can turn out to be a bit deceptive in our deepest intentions.

In all truth, some of us never quite reach the deepest level five, even though it's the most important stage and the one we should shoot for. It involves total focus and absorption in what our partner is saying. Getting there is exceptionally rare and hard to maintain. But in order to drive communication in a relationship forward, it's vital that we try to achieve that deepest level.

Here, then, are the levels we're talking about:

- Ignoring

- Pretend listening

- Selective listening

- Attentive listening

- Empathetic listening

1. Ignoring

I'm betting this level is obvious: it's not listening at all—an ostrich with its head in the sand. Whether you're distracted, consumed with something else, or flat-out don't care, ignoring is an immediate discouragement to anyone who's trying to speak to you.

> *Person A:* I'm worried about our son. He's spending an awful lot of time online and doesn't interact with anyone in the real world anymore.
>
> *Person B:*

Person A: It's like he's got no interest in forming real relationships with anybody. It's got me quite concerned.

Person B:

Person A: Hello?

Person B:

Person A: Also, he just drove our minivan into the river and is sacrificing animals to the Dark Lord in our living room.

Person B:

Person A: Are you hearing a word I'm saying?

Person B: Hey, look at that squirrel!

There's not much to be said about this level. It's bad communication at its worst. Person B is utterly uninterested in Person A's point of view and makes no effort to say anything until something catches their personal interest. This first level of communication is important to get out of ASAP. (But keep in mind, someone not being *able* to hear you is not ignoring, so speak up if you can.)

2. Pretend Listening

This happens most prevalently in face-to-face communication. We *look* like we're paying attention, but we're not entirely engaged with what our partner is saying. Our eyes might get that distant look, and we just don't appear to be "all there." We make the slightest cues imaginable just to appear that we're taking everything in. But in reality, we're kind of phoning it in, like a bored hall monitor. This isn't even about different listening styles or frames, unless your frame for the conversation is to placate someone and be a fake friend.

> *Person A:* I had a talk with my sister the other day. Her husband's been staying long hours at the office. I think she suspects something.
>
> *Person B:* Mm-hmm.
>
> *Person A:* I mean, I know she can get a little overly dramatic and unduly suspicious. But he can't have that much work to do. Not so much that he misses four dinners a week.
>
> *Person B:* Yes.

Person A: I kind of think she might have cause for concern. Don't you?

Person B: Yeah. Wait, what?

Person A: Have you really heard anything I'm saying?

Person B: Uh... hey, look. That squirrel's back again.

The level two listener is making only a superficial effort to convince their partner that they're involved in the conversation so as not to appear rude. But of course, they're still preoccupied with their own thoughts and concerns. They stay at the minimum baseline, and it can be frustrating to anyone trying to impart a real thought or concern. It's progress, but not much.

3. Selective Listening

At this level we start to give our partner real attention—to a point. As long as the speaker is saying something we agree or sympathize with, we're with them. But if they switch direction and put forth an idea that doesn't jibe with us, we go back to pretend listening or ignoring them. It can be a reaction to a sentiment we have resistance toward, a story we don't care about, or a statement we disagree with. We initially sound like we're involved and concerned, but at a certain breakpoint we retreat under our shell of self-absorption.

> *Person A:* I've had it up to here with the people at work. It's the refrigerator policy. I've said for weeks that if your name is on a container, it should be untouchable.

> *Person B:* I agree with you. People are still stealing your food?

> *Person A:* Yes. Someone is using my salad dressing.

> *Person B:* Oh, that's not good.

> *Person A:* I get what they're thinking. They think salad dressing is not really a piece of food. They think it's more like a condiment. Like mustard and ketchup.

> *Person B:* I guess I understand why people would think that way. You're only supposed to use a little bit of

ketchup or mustard on something, whereas with salad dressing you probably use more at a time.

Person A: You know what? Even if there *is* a bottle of ketchup in the fridge, if *my* name is on that bottle, it's untouchable. If I feel like sharing my ketchup, I'll offer some.

Person B: But it's just ketchup.

Person A: So what? If my name is on it, the ketchup's off limits to anyone but me. If you need ketchup so badly, then hop over to the fast-food joint and take a bunch of those ketchup packets. Leave mine alone.

Person B:

Person A: It's just the kind of disrespect that's so typical of how we live today! They think we should just throw ketchup around like it's something they're *entitled* to! I don't care! If I've declared that it's mine, you have to *ask* if you want to use it! You know?

Person B:

Person A: I said, "YOU KNOW?"

Person B: Oh, sorry. I was just looking at a squirrel on TV.

First, don't worry about how silly this exchange might sound. I made it silly on purpose. Person A is upset about something that many might consider a terribly trivial, "first-world" problem. They're tired of a certain pattern and it's driving them crazy. Is it even worth the breath to complain about it?

The answer… doesn't matter. Whatever we think of Person A's obsession with ownership of foodstuffs, they're *upset* about what's happening. There is nothing wrong with feeling that way. It's Person A's feelings and they're entitled to feel any way they want about the refrigerator situation.

Person B agrees with Person A to a point. But then Person A says something that Person B doesn't agree with: that salad dressing and ketchup are, for all intents and purposes, not equals in the world of refrigerator leftovers. Person B thinks

Person A's making a ridiculous point and has tuned them out.

Even if we *agree* with Person B and disagree with Person A, the fact is that when the conversation took a turn that Person B didn't like, they reverted to level-one ignoring of Person A. They just dropped out and stopped listening altogether.

That's selective listening: when the talk's going our way and resounding with our values, everything's great. But when we hear something that strikes us as wrong, we check out. It doesn't matter whether the topic is ketchup, world politics, family matters, or death—selective listening is still an incomplete level of communication (and some might consider it worse than ignoring, since it creates a false impression of involvement).

4. Attentive Listening

This, in all honesty, is good. Not perfect but good. We're giving our partner our complete attention and listening to every detail they provide. We're not distracted, we're not shutting them out selectively, and we're not changing the subject.

However, what keeps this level from being five-star, fully focused listening is our analytical and judgmental mind. While the other person speaks, we're comparing their statements to our own points of view, deciding whether we're in agreement with them or not, like someone on a debate team. This is more than fair in a two-way conversation where both parties are expected to provide equal exchange. But the fact that we're still assessing our partner with our own reason and logic keeps it from becoming pure listening:

> *Person A:* My mother is starting an online business.
>
> *Person B:* Doing what?
>
> *Person A:* Selling some of her homemade crafts. She thinks she can do it on her own. I'm not sure she's completely aware of what she's in for.
>
> *Person B:* What are your doubts?

Person A: That she's never done anything remotely related to web management or coding, and I don't know that she knows anyone who has. She's almost seventy and I'm just concerned she's underestimating what it will take.

Person B: You know, there are relatively cheap courses she can take online that can teach her to do it from scratch. It's helped a lot of people.

Person A: Yeah, I suppose she can look into those.

As you can see, this last exchange doesn't end in a disagreement, an invalidation, detachment, or, thankfully, another squirrel sighting. It's a fair and open exchange. Person B is paying close attention to what Person A says and is drawing Person A out so they feel safe to reveal their innermost feelings. That's all good.

But after hearing Person A explain what their doubts are, Person B makes a suggestion that Person A's mom check out some online courses. Person B made this recommendation from their *own* standpoint. Hearing Person A's doubts activated Person B's own experience, judgment, or opinion, and it caused Person B to make a remark that was on topic but not reflective of what Person A was thinking or feeling.

Is this terrible? Of course not. Maybe Person A and Person B talk this way with each other all the time. They might be perfectly comfortable with giving and hearing each other's advice and might even welcome it. But Person A *could* have taken Person B's suggestion as a form of invalidation. Person A was in the midst of expressing her emotional state and may not have been finished—they could have interpreted Person B's advice as a forced solution intended to stop the conversation.

It all depends on how secure and close their relationship is and what boundaries they've set up for themselves in communication. Attentive listening is very good. Responses like Person B's aren't criminal and hopefully don't result in a spell of eggshell-walking when they're trying to figure out what to say. These potentially invalidating responses are just something to be aware of, think about, and consider in advance of the communication.

5. Empathetic Listening

This is both the final, most desirable level of listening and the polar opposite of the first level of ignoring. In empathetic listening we give all our attention to the person we're talking to. We're not just zeroed in on what they're saying—we're putting ourselves in their shoes. We're not theorizing what *we* would do or feel in their situation; we're making a strong effort to understand where they're coming from.

In empathetic listening we react as though we're hearing our partner's story for the first time, even if it's something we've talked about before. We treat it as new and unusual information that doesn't pass through our own judgments, values, opinions, or frames of reference. It's not an easy level to achieve and requires discipline. But it's the most rewarding for both conversation partners.

Person A: I know we've talked about this before, but Chris is really getting to me. He's been impossible to deal with the last couple of weeks and I'm not sure what to do about it.

Person B: What is happening?

Person A: He's remote. He's emotionally distant. He's been staying out late most nights, and when he doesn't he locks himself into his study and shuts himself off.

Person B: You must feel extremely lonely.

Person A: Yeah, but more to the point, I just feel like I've been left out to dry. We've been together seven years and this sudden change just came out of nowhere. I'm confused. I don't know what brought it on. I don't know if he's hiding something from me or whether this is just what longtime couples go through.

Person B: You must be struggling to endure under that kind of mystery.

Person A: Yeah, I am. If I could get any clarity from him on the situation, it would be helpful. I don't know; we'll see.

In this example, Person B takes themselves out of the story completely. They start off by prompting Person A to confide in them. Then they try to imagine the emotional and mental state Person A is going through without making themselves the subject.

That's why Person B says, *"You must feel extremely lonely"* rather than *"I would feel extremely lonely"*—a small, maybe imperceptible difference in syntax, but one that reinforces that Person A is the subject of the exchange and that Person B is giving them their full focus.

Then Person B imagines being in Person A's position and tries to empathize: "You must be struggling to endure under that kind of mystery." This shows that Person B is really trying to understand what Person A is going through. That's different from the step in level four, in which one compares what they're hearing with their own experience and judgments—it's a *guess*, not a declaration. And it's a "You" statement, not an "I" statement. That reminds Person A that they're getting full attention and comprehension, which in itself is a validating and positive communication experience.

Takeaways:

- Let's suppose you're trying to learn how to play the guitar. You're right-handed, but you've accidentally gone and bought a guitar for left-handers. This is not a recipe for success. That's how we can think about the different types of listening styles that exist. We must match our style with that of other people if we are to have any hope for success.

- Though it can be said there are countless listening styles, it's helpful to think in terms of four main styles: people (emotion), content (information), action (to-do list), and time (duration and frequency) orientations. For our purposes, we want to recognize which is our natural tendency, and then try to skew more toward the people/emotion style. This is because when people communicate outside of giving an order or organizing an outing, they are doing so to express an emotion. Go find it! Another way to delineate listening styles is to think in terms of head, heart, and hands. Head is all about thinking and planning, hands is all about doing and action, and the heart, well, that's all about emotion and people's well-being. Again, recognize where you are, and how to move toward people/emotion/heart styles of listening.

- Frames are a different way to imagine listening styles. Frames are much more fluid, and simply ask you to consider what someone's overall goals or purpose for the interaction is. What is theirs, what is yours, and do they match? If not, utilize your new understanding and make them match. An easy way to think about frames is in terms of an acting scene. All the actors are on the same page, working toward the same goal, and trying to capture an emotional payoff. What happens if one of the actors wants to wing it for a bit, and expound on their character's love of the sea? Nothing good.

- Finally, we get to levels of listening. Unlike listening frames and styles, some of these levels of listening are just plain bad. The levels are: ignoring, pretending to listen, selectively listening, attentively listening, and empathetically listening. The first two levels are not very useful, and it's only when we reach the ultimate level of empathetically listening that we remove ourselves from the equation and listen to hear rather than listen to reply. Most of us are stuck in the first three to four levels for the majority of our day-to-day interactions.

Chapter 3. The Tough Work of Hearing Someone

Two people are in a coffee shop, "catching up" after a long time not chatting, and discussing this and that.

Ted: "I've tried to talk to him so many times about it, but I have to say, he doesn't really seem to *get* it, you know?"
Kristen: "Well—what do you mean? What doesn't he get?"

Ted: "It's like... I heard someone say once that a woman becomes a mother the moment she knows she's pregnant, but a man only becomes a dad once the baby is born. I feel like that. Like maybe he's not caught up yet..."

Kristen: "Like he's not on the same page as you…"

Ted: "Exactly. And I feel like it's all still just abstract for him, like it hasn't really sunk in yet. I mean, I sympathize, but, I don't know…"

Kristen: "Oh, I hear you. Seems like you sympathize but there's also something else."

Ted: "There is. I guess I'm a bit disappointed? Maybe I'm just scared that I'm actually going to be doing this all by myself, and that's not what we agreed to. That's *not* what I thought we were doing. We're a team."

Kristen: "You thought you guys were… kind of in this together."

Ted: "Yes. But when I talk to him… it doesn't feel like that. Like he's kind of making it like *I'm* pregnant and he's just kind of a spectator. I mean, I don't want to speak badly about him…"

Kristen: "Of course not! It seems like this is not an easy thing to talk about."

Ted: "Well what could I say? I think deep down I'm just… he can leave at this point, you know? And I'm the one that's *really* doing this. Does that make sense?"

Kristen: "Oh, completely. Do you think it's that you're worried about him leaving?"

And so on. In the above conversation, both people are spending almost equal time talking, yet one person is definitely speaking and expressing while the other is definitely listening—actively. If you go back and look at the conversation again, you'll see that the listener is more or less repeating the same content back to the speaker, albeit rephrasing the information, sometimes framing it as a question, or simply offering encouragement and support ("Oh, I hear you").

Not much is actually being said, but it's eliciting a large response and a certain kind of elaboration that shows comfort and emotional fulfillment. The key is that the speaker can truly feel they are being heard, and this is part of what we do when we're listening—not just staying silent.

The speaker in this conversation likely feels extraordinarily heard and supported in this conversation. The other person is giving them their complete attention, not merely hearing but engaging deeply with the content—both factual and emotional—of what's being said. Instead of interjecting with their own ideas, however, the listener is skillfully reflecting and summarizing what they've been told. Importantly, this is not just parroting what has been said, word for word. The listener also occasionally "tests" their comprehension—"it sounds like you mean such-and-such, is that the case? Have I understood?"

This communicates loud and clear that the listener's goal in the conversation is to understand the speaker deeply. In fact, it's almost as though the listener is actively helping the speaker make their point, using cues and guiding them along. Such conversations can often lead to deeper insights and understandings, the kind of talk that leaves people feeling understood, connected, and like they've actively tackled some problem or issue. You may feel like you are giving someone your full attention, but unless you're participating in a way that makes them feel this attention, then it's as good as not happening.

This is the "big talk" (versus small talk) that brings people closer together. When two good conversationalists encounter one another, they can take turns actively listening, and rather than the conversation being an exercise in ego, attention seeking, arguing or petty small talk, it becomes a platform to establish meaningful connections, enjoy the company of another person, solve problems, and dig into the juicy topics of life.

Perhaps the above conversation reminded you of what a good psychologist might do, and indeed this method was explored in depth by the famous psychologist Carl Rogers. He believed that "unconditional positive regard" in a therapeutic encounter as well as active listening, empathy and reflection were the keys to truly transformative conversations—and therapy is, in the end, simply a kind of conversation.

Listening is not passive. Many people resist listening because they frame it as an unwanted relinquishing of the stage, as a boring side role in the story, where they have to "sit out" and wait for the other person to give them an in. This is a disastrous mindset, because conversations only work when both people are actively, consciously involved. The mistake is to think that talking is somehow more interesting or more active than listening. Nothing could be further from the truth. And again, taking the spotlight is a completely different goal from connecting with someone else.

Exceptional listeners know something that poor listeners don't—that it is just as enjoyable to hear someone else talk and share as it is to talk, maybe even more so at times. It can be just as satisfying, if not more, to crack someone open like a nut, and get true emotion and expression flowing. The work involved also doesn't have to be as boring as sitting quietly and nodding your head. It can be quite active, and almost like unraveling a riddle—if you can only use the right responses. That's exactly what active listening is.

Active Listening

We talked in the previous chapter about the five levels of listening. How do we reach the ultimate level? Just as learning to read and write takes practice, so does the art of active listening.

Active listening is one of the strongest relationship-building skills you can have in your arsenal. It establishes respect and concern for your partner's viewpoints and makes it easier for you to process information that's intricate and difficult to understand through passive listening. It also eases the communication process: active listening helps you learn what the other person's needs are, and therefore makes you less cautious and more open with your responses.

Perhaps above all else, active listening makes it 100 percent clear and certain that you *are* comprehending your conversation partner. They know that you're right there with them.

At the same time, we have to push our ego out of the way so we can truly access what the other person is saying. We call this process "active" listening because it engages so many parts of our mind and makes us *do* something to understand what's being communicated.

Therapists (good ones, at least, unlike the one mentioned earlier in this book) are excellent models of how to be an active listener. They listen to their clients with a clear purpose. If there's something they're hearing that they're not 100 percent sure about, they encourage their clients to be clear and deliberate.

These therapists try to restate their patients' statements and ask them to elaborate on what they mean. Above all, they try to make their clients feel calm and safe about communicating through contemplation, clear body language, and a spirit of empathy. Therapists are driven by a very clear goal of hearing their clients out, and their every response is informed by this goal. Can we say the same about ourselves when we are trying to listen to others?

Active listening involves a few essential types of reactions and inquiries that you can start using almost immediately. These are all designed to ensure that the speaker can *feel* you are on the same emotional page as them. After all, what's listening if it's only going on inside your head, and not being conveyed to the other person?

Comprehending. The first step in active listening is, of course, comprehending what the other person is saying in the first place. If the person who's talking to us is speaking the same language as we normally do, this process is fairly automatic.

But there are other potential blocks—for example, if the person uses a lot of jargon or slang that we aren't familiar with or if there are differences in generation, social standing, or culture that we just don't know enough about. Above all else, you just want to make sure you are on the same emotional page as the speaker, so you can ascertain their needs and desires at the moment.

A great thing to ask if we're not understanding what someone's saying is

"Can you explain it to me as if I were five years old?" A five-year-old knows enough words to hold a conversation but needs to have relatively complex situations described to them in a very patient, deliberate way using the words they already know. Especially if you think the other person fears appearing condescending or patronizing, asking them to describe something as if you were, let's say, *far younger than your actual age,* can make them feel a little more at ease.

Other statements to ask for help comprehending include:

- "What happened?"

- "Tell me your story."

- "What do you mean?"

- "Tell me more."

- "Can you clear this part up for me?"

Retaining. More than just remembering what you just heard, retaining information is hearing what the speaker is trying to say so we can give back a suitable reply. You're trying to get the whole story here, and this goes far beyond simple facts and events. The goal is to place yourself in the speaker's shoes as closely as possible, and of course, questions are necessary for that.

When we're listening to someone, we tend to retain only the details that strike us more personally or in ways that we're most used to retaining information. But that's only our lens, and not particularly useful for trying to be a better listener.

For example, if someone's telling us about a date they went on, we might be the kind who remembers the physical details of the event (what restaurant they went to, what movie they saw, what they were wearing). Or we might recall some more general narrative about the date as a whole (what personality the other person had, what the date "felt like," how it compared to other dates in the past).

In conversation we generally look for openings for us to say something and "get our two cents in." This is normal, but it's not conducive to active listening. To properly retain what our conversation partner is telling us, we have to put our egos away and focus squarely on the other person's words.

To ensure you're retaining all the relevant information you need, you could ask:

- "What does that mean to you?"

- "And just to be clear, what happened after?"

- "Wait, how did she approach that?"

- "How does that figure into the story?"

- "How did that make you feel?"

- "What was your reaction?"

Responding. Active listening requires an effort to form a knowing and proper response—otherwise, the speaker might feel like they're talking to a brick wall. As has been said multiple times, listening is anything *but* passive! An effective response will demonstrate our concern for what our conversation partner is talking about.

You're listening, comprehending, and retaining already; a quality response will prove that you *understand* everything the speaker has said and picked up on their nonverbal communication. Imagine that you are speaking to someone, and you're not sure that they understand the language you are speaking. They give no indication of comprehension—do you feel listened to? That's why a response is necessary.

Like retaining, it's important that a response isn't tinted with our own ego or ideas. You're trying to get a sense of the other person's feelings and opinions without biases you've developed:

> *Speaker A:* And that's why I don't like going to dinner parties.
>
> *Respondent B:* That sounds insane! Were you flustered when that odd man jumped out of the cake?
>
> *Speaker A:* Not flustered so much as disappointed. I expected something a little more grown-up from the Temperance League.
>
> *Respondent B:* It must have tried your patience. Did it?

Speaker A: A little bit. But more than anything else, it just proved that I have to start putting some restrictions on the entertainment budget.

Responses in active listening should be reflective of what the speaker has said. They should display a deep interest in your partner's thoughts and feelings. Rather than expressing our *own* opinions and viewpoints, good responses in active listening help both parties make their own self-discoveries.

In issuing a quality response, try to reply to your partner's thoughts and feelings. You can do this by restating what they've said in your own words. Stay within their standpoint when you respond; introducing a suggestion or idea that doesn't have anything to do with their immediate situation could be too jarring or distracting. Don't offer a contradictory or conflicting opinion until you have fully understood, as much as you can, everything your partner is conveying to you. And even then, try to keep strong judgments tamped down.

Some positive responses in active listening might be:

- "I'm intrigued by your story."

- "That sounds like a ____ situation."

- "I can see how you'd feel that way."

- "I get the sense that you feel something has to change—what would you like to see happen?"

- "Do you feel ____ about this situation?"

The general goal of active listening is to fully grasp the viewpoint or life experience of the person who's speaking to you, and for you to absorb that information in a meaningful way that could spur you to new knowledge and understanding. To accomplish the goals of comprehending, retaining, and responding, you can employ a few or more of these techniques:

Restating. Paraphrasing your partner's sentiments in your own words is an exceptional way to facilitate your comprehension. It's important *not* to simply repeat what they said back to them like a parrot, but rather to show that you've caught the essence of what they were expressing. You're letting them know that you heard them and are on the same page with them. If you're not 100 percent right, they will almost certainly be sure to correct you.

> *Them:* That situation confused and scared me.

> *You:* It must have felt like a dangerous moment—it must have been hard to know what to do.

Reflecting. An alternative way of restating is to frame your reply along the lines of emotions rather than events or story points. Reflecting gives the speaker's story a deeper level that you can prove you have a handle on. Literally tell them, or ask them, about the emotion they are experiencing.

> *Them:* So in the end, my dad said he knew all along I wouldn't get into that college.

> *You:* That's terrible. That sounds like a cruel kind of rejection.

Summarizing. Try to verbally round up the details of a speaker's story into a concise form that displays your grasp of the whole picture. This is similar to restating, but you are going for a broader overview. You can also treat this as a test for your understanding. Many points and arguments may have been stated, and you may have lost sight of the primary emotion, action, or purpose.

> *You:* So the baker got your order wrong, the dinner was burned, and they sent a hypnotist instead of a clown. Man, if that were *my* kid's birthday party, I'd feel ticked off!

Label emotions. Often, a speaker will get lost in the practical and physical details of what they're relating to you. As sensitively as possible, try to identify the emotions they haven't been able to specifically verbalize yet. This is not inherently difficult to do, as you only have to state a type of positive or negative feeling, but when you accurately label someone's emotion, you are going to be seen as a psychic.

> *Them:* Finally my boss apologized for overlooking my work and assured me that he was going to pay more attention from now on.

> *You:* Wow, I'm guessing you feel pretty relieved and vindicated by that—not to mention a little cocky.

Probing. Without sounding like an invasive interrogator, try to ask leading questions that will elicit a deeper level of understanding and meaning from the person you're speaking with. Most people enjoy being asked questions that are well-formed and not too presumptuous. When you probe, you can try to make guesses at how people feel, their reactions and desires. This type of forecasting shows that you are so engaged you want to jump to conclusions with them, and keep riding their train of thought. You're not only there with them, you're caught up in their emotions.

> *You:* What did it feel like when that woman berated your kid at the supermarket? How did you *really* want to respond?

Silence. Frequently there's more to be said by a well-placed silence than by filling up the space with additional verbiage. Silence can give every participant a miniature moment of time to gather themselves and their thoughts. It could also help reduce the tension that could arise from a heated or fruitless interaction.

> *Them:* And *that's* when I decided skydiving wasn't my thing, especially when it's work-related.
>
> *You:*

<u>Not</u> *sermonizing, giving unsolicited advice, or glibly reassuring.* Nobody likes to be put on a level secondary to someone else, and in communication, this might make the speaker feel like shutting down further discussion.

> *Them:* And worst of all, he cannot remember to put the toilet seat down.
>
> *Sermonizing you:* You should never have let him in your bathroom in the first place.

Unsolicited advising you: You should barricade the bathroom until he agrees to your demands.

Glibly reassuring you: Don't worry about it! Tomorrow's another lovely day full of wonderful possibilities.

Asking leading and open-ended questions. To show that you're invested in your partner's well-being, ask some nonbinary questions about their experience. These questions show that you're ready to get input and that you're interested in more than just the data or facts of a certain situation.

Them: So I decided, a couple hundred dollars later, perhaps parallel parking was something we were going to have to work a little harder on.

You: How does that make you feel? What are your plans for learning? Where do you plan on doing it? What do you hope comes out of it?

Active listening takes a lot of patient work and practice and can even be challenging for people who are good at it. But it pays off in creating an atmosphere of true comprehension, easier information flow, and increased respect for all parties. What we are trying to do, albeit systematically, with active listening is to catch the habit of being conscious of other people's emotions and suppressing our own. The ultimate form of this comes in empathetic reflection.

Empathetic Reflection

Empathy in dialogue comes from embodying the other person's point of view—and showing it. As you listen, engage. Continually ask yourself, internally, what is being said, and how, and why. If something appears to be unreasonable or illogical, it's not because you are talking to an unreasonable or illogical person—you are just missing part of the equation in that person's train of thought. This comes more naturally to some than others, but you can practice by saying things like the following:

- "That makes sense."
- "Hmm, can you say more about XYZ? What did you mean when you said ABC?"

- "It seems like such-and-so is the case. Have I understood you properly?"
- "Uh-huh. I get that."
- "Go on."
- "Do you think that (insert tentative interpretation)?"
- "I'm really curious about (something they've said earlier)…"
- "Oh wow. Well done!"
- "So why did you XYZ?"
- "What happened then?"
- "So, you're telling me (very quick summary of what was just said)?"

Be warned, however, that your active listening techniques can be utterly abused by a conversational narcissist, who will only need the slightest encouragement. In this case, sit back and listen as much as you can handle, and gracefully bow out if you can—you can't "win" at being more cooperative with a person who is determined to dominate. Smile and practice your empathetic listening skills—you'll be glad you did when a more cooperative conversation partner does turn up!

Picture the above conversation again, but with a poor conversationalist.

"I've tried to talk to him so many times about it, but I have to say, he doesn't really seem to *get* it, you know?"
(Silence).
"Ugh, I don't know. I feel like maybe I shouldn't complain."
(Disinterested nod as the person quickly glances at their phone screen).
"Anyway, enough about me, I guess. How are you and Mike?"
(Suddenly animated) "Oh, we're great. The other day we went to this really amazing concert, did I tell you about it? So, what happened was...*blah blah blah.*"

Later, the original speaker battles to "get a word in edgeways" and what follows is a ho-hum, hour-long chat about various concerts around the city.

What could have been a quite intimate, connecting conversation that really benefitted both parties has simply become a shared soapbox that each member is invited to take turns standing on and relating their story. If you've ever found someone boring, it might be because they were in fact *bored*—i.e. with you and what you had to say, and unable to express any curiosity or interest in *you*.

It bears remembering this when you think about how you can become a better conversationalist yourself. Try to think of why some conversations have left you feeling ignored, misunderstood or not really heard—what was the other person's attitude to you? Perhaps we can put our own "narcissism" to good use here. To be good listeners, we need to give other people the opportunity to speak, be heard, take up space with their stories—i.e., what we want when we're tempted to butt into or dominate conversations!

Think of it as being reflective—not absorbing a story so much as bouncing it back to the speaker, like in our proverbial game of tennis. You may have encountered this when interacting with a very young child. When babies are very little, they have to learn about who they are, what they're feeling, and what their experiences mean.

A mother might look at a crying child and mimic his frowning expression, saying, "Aw, are you unhappy about that?" Essentially, by doing this, she teaches the child that his emotion is called "unhappy" and even though he can't quite understand it in himself, he can see the expression on *her* face, and begin to make sense of his own experience.

In other words, empathetic reflection helps people deepen and comprehend their own experience. It's why it's so important to be "witnessed" in so many areas of life, why we need an audience at times, why we need others to give us their attention—in a very deep way, it confirms what we are feeling, and even deeper still, confirms that we simply exist.

Developmental disruptions to this reflective process are thought to play a part in narcissism in later life—a person may eternally seek external validation, seeing other people not as independent beings of their own, but merely as tools to confirm their own ego (mirrors!), or as supporting parts in a grand play where they are the main and possibly only character.

When we dig deep, we can see that conversation is not merely the exchange of information, but can express many important things about who we are and want to be, how we need to be seen and acknowledged by others, and even how we need other people to help us define ourselves and our experiences—by listening.

Have you ever felt that really opening up to someone has helped you better understand your predicament? Try to offer the same to the next person you want to truly listen to. Adopt an approach of, "I see you. What you are saying and feeling is important, and so are you." Isn't it funny how so many of us crave this attention and validation, all the while being utterly unwilling to extend the same courtesy to others?

From this basic attitude, it becomes much easier to genuinely engage with a person, rather than learning a set of techniques and phrases and hoping that using them will inspire you to become a better listener from the outside in. It might be a fun challenge to train yourself to really take your ego out of things.

Try for one whole day to dedicate yourself to only listening to others. Become a passionate and curious researcher of the human condition. Extend the warmest, most fascinated attention to the people you engage with. You may find, counterintuitively, that you are far more liked than if you had set out to impress people deliberately!

Another approach is to imagine that both you and the other person are not key players, but rather that the conversation itself is what's most important. View both conversation partners as midwives, together helping birth into being a more refined, better-understood idea, a new thought, or a refreshed sense of rapport and connection. Hear what you're being told, send it back and add a little extra "interest" (pun intended) to show you valued the original investment. Encourage your conversation partner to come along with you on this fascinating process of building a thing you own together.

You can add to the conversation in many ways. Try extrapolating—taking what's been said and extending the idea, asking about what happens next or following an idea to its natural conclusion:

"Well, I'm fed up with teaching and I certainly don't want to go back to my old job either..."
"Does that mean you're thinking of doing something completely different then?"

You can also add by synthesizing—taking separate ideas and combining them thoughtfully. The idea is that the whole would be greater than the sum of the parts—i.e., you're adding a bigger picture that's more valuable than simply considering each point in isolation. A good way to do this is to abandon either/or thinking and consider "this AND that" thinking:

"Well, I've got my mother on the one hand telling me one thing, and my friends telling

me to do another, and I don't have a clue who to listen to!"
"Have you considered that you don't have to listen to either of them?"

Reflecting is also both a cause and an effect of creating an emotional bond with someone. By using the same words, imagery, or tone of voice, you're showing the speaker that you're on "their side" and care about building a bridge between you.

"This lesson really sucks, seriously." (Spoken by a teenaged student to her adult teacher).
"*Does it*? Well what sucks about it?"

Using the same language creates so much more of a rapport than saying something like, "If you're dissatisfied with the lesson, maybe you'd like to take up the matter with the principal." Responding to a casual tone with a formal and stilted one only serves to highlight distance, and is unlikely to lead to any sense of shared goals in this particular dialogue!

Of course, reflecting doesn't only have to be verbal. A person telling you a sad story with a slow, somber tone of voice will likely appreciate if you match them, rather than talking back to them loudly and excitedly. Similarly, body language can say a lot, as can facial expressions. Much can be communicated by simply adopting a similar posture when talking to someone. If they lean in, lean in a little too, to show your nonverbal agreement. If they're smiling as they recount a particular part of their story, smiling along with them is the nonverbal equivalent of saying "uh-huh" and shows that you understand and empathize.

Some people may even consider slightly changing pitch of voice or accent to highlight what is common between the two parties (or to emphasize how uncommon you are, if that's what you want to do!). Have you ever noticed how two expats from the same country will sometimes overemphasize their native accent when talking to one another? They are unconsciously signaling to the other, "I'm like you. We're friends, we're on the same page." However, notice as well that if someone has been living in a foreign country for decades but steadfastly refuses to use the local dialect ("it's called a sofa, not a couch!"), it certainly tells you something.

A woman might unconsciously simplify her grammar and raise her voice's pitch when talking to small children, but throw in plenty of big, impressive words and talk more deeply when speaking to senior men in a corporate environment. A doctor might choose to use the Latin term for a common ailment specifically because he wants to distinguish himself as more intelligent and important than his non-medical audience. Conversational empathy is ultimately about so much more than the literal words that are being spoken.

Bearing all this in mind, however, it's worth remembering that reflecting might not always be the best idea, and can go wrong. If you reflect back something inaccurate, you may unintentionally show that you weren't listening properly, with unfortunate consequences. This can usually be fixed by a sincere request for more information or an apology, but the best approach is to take baby steps and avoid sweeping interpretations of what you're being told. Nobody likes to feel like they're being analyzed, or being told what they think!

Another risk is "premature exposure," which is bringing up something the other person is not comfortable discussing, or ready to explore yet—with you or maybe with anyone. In the conversation at the start of this section, a particularly astute listener may say, "I wonder if you're reconsidering your relationship with this guy." This comment may be "true" in some sense, but a little too close to home and way more intimate than the speaker may be bargaining for. If this happens, a respectful backtrack can help. Change the subject, or use a little humor to transition gracefully away from the sensitive topic.

"Emotional abandonment" is another thing to watch out for. Let's say you made the above statement, and the other person, trusting you, runs with it. They may open up further, share some personal details, and make themselves rather vulnerable. If you nod and listen, then suggest you get a coffee and bluntly change the topic, they may feel abandoned, as though you led them out into deep water and just left them there, feeling exposed. Psychologists who goad clients into gut-wrenching territory only to cheerfully tell them their session is finished, before quickly escorting the person out of the room with tears still on their face—this is emotional abandonment!

Finally, we should all remember that being a good listener *doesn't* mean playing shrink to someone, and that we can go too far psychologizing someone or attempting to make grand theories and explanations of how they feel that just don't resonate with them. Don't mind-read, don't assume, and don't project your own story onto others— this will not feel like empathy, it will feel like an intrusion.

In listening, you want to travel alongside people as they reach their own conclusions, rather than assuming that you are wise and all-knowing and can *show* them something. Offer names for emotions or gently suggest possible connections or interpretations, but use a light touch. Don't say things like, "This is just so typical of you. You have a *type*, and you're always going after the same type of guy because of your father issues, right? I bet you're so angry right now." Instead, say, "Gosh, I can't even imagine what that feels like for you. What do you make of all this, though?"

Some of the world's worst conversationalists are those who wrongly believe they are good listeners, and who unconsciously use "empathy" to dominate a conversation and indirectly feed their ego. Don't fall into this trap!

Takeaways:

- Listening is a truly not a passive activity. Well, it can be, but that would just mean that you're not doing a good job. True, deep listening can be said to be extremely active, to the point of tiring you out! Surprised? This is because the purpose of true, deep listening is to *go there* with someone, and this involves teasing out exactly where you are even heading. It's a job that requires a lot of comprehension, solving subtle mysteries, and clarification. It's a bit like a therapist's role in helping unravel emotions and situations.

- To this end, we come to the concept of active listening. It's a way to participate in conversations while being on the receiving end. Most might think that receiving simply means sitting quietly, but that's a huge mistake. There are nine types of active listening responses we cover, to be used when trying to connect deeply with someone: comprehending, retaining, responding, restating, reflecting, summarizing, labeling emotions, probing with leading questions, and silence. The next level of active listening could be called empathetic reflection, and this is where the listener focuses on emotion, so much so that you are trying to predict what the speaker is feeling, and share it with them.

Chapter 4. I See You, I Hear You

Going deeper than conversation styles, specific words you say and so on, we arrive at perhaps the deepest function of any communication—to be seen, heard, understood and acknowledged by another person, and to do the same for them. Listening without judgment, without trying to "fix" anything or change how another person feels, and without rushing in with your own feelings on the matter—all this comes from having empathy.

True empathy diffuses conflict and encourages deeper intimacy. So-called "non-violent communication" is based on the principle of seeking to understand a person's emotional reality, rather than deny it, change it, judge it, praise it, explain it away or take responsibility for it. As amazing as this sounds, it does take practice, however. Consider the following conversation.

Unnecessary Input

"I miss her so much. I know I'm supposed to be over it already, but I guess when she passed I sort of just went on hold somehow, and I only feel like I'm processing things now..."
"Sounds like you're having a hard time."

"Yeah. I don't know. Some days it's OK, but to be honest I'm not really coping with this."
"Hm, I remember when my mom died, I was a mess for a year. But looking back it was kind of a good thing too, in some ways, you know?"

"A good thing?"
"I just learnt so much about myself, going through all that."

"I guess."

"You should come to kickboxing with me, I found it really helps to do something physical, get the blood pumping again!"

"Maybe... I kind of feel like moping for a while to be honest."
"Hey... chin up. I know how you feel. Just remind yourself of the good times, right? You're doing so well, I'm proud of you for trying to stay positive through all this. I don't know, life works in mysterious ways sometimes..."

Though both people may leave this conversation feeling like the listener was being empathetic and trying their best to be helpful, the speaker likely never felt truly *heard*. When we care about someone, it can be heard to really hear and acknowledge their "negative" emotions, and we may not even notice ourselves jumping in to fix and solve, to explain away. Though the intentions may be good, the unconscious communication is: *how you feel is not valid.*

The listener above offers advice, and tries to cheer up the speaker with glib suggestions, as though they were standing far off from the speaker's pain, unwilling to really acknowledge it or get too close. The relentless focus on positivity ironically only emphasizes the negativity—and the speaker may feel sadder and more alone after this conversation than they did before.

To use empathy wisely, try to listen without judgment—easier said than done. Don't interpret or explain, don't theorize or justify. Don't take responsibility for making the other person feel better, don't blame, don't feel guilty. You might ask: well, what's left to do? That's simple: just listen and accept what is being said.

Be curious about what's actually being communicated, take your ego out of the picture for a while, and simply witness what's being said, without rushing through the conversation. Be present and try to *understand* where the speaker is coming from, emotionally. If anything else needs to be addressed, the time will come, but we usually want to leap ahead a few steps in the process and that leads to the feeling of being unheard.

Don't get stuck on the facts or the logical argument of what's being presented, but listen instead with your "heart" and hear the emotional content. How is the speaker feeling? What are their desires, fears, needs? Completely forget about who is right and who is to blame. "Get into the hole" with them, alongside them. You don't have to become overwhelmed with their emotions, but you can certainly try to see things through their eyes for a while. True understanding can feel so much better than advice or problem-solving—which often just misses the point.

To be an empathic communicator is to be emotionally mature in yourself and comfortable with emotions, whatever they are. It's the ability to be vulnerable enough to feel, rather than run away from feelings, grasp at solutions or avoid discomfort at all costs. In fact, the better you're able to tolerate your own discomfort without rushing in to fix or deny it, the more you'll be able to offer this to others.

When people are grieving, they sometimes say how they're doubly saddened by people's awkward and avoidant responses to their grief. What they really want in the moment is to have their reality mirrored to them honestly and fearlessly. They want someone to say, "That hurts. I can see it hurts" and simply be with them, letting them know they are not alone.

A good habit to get into is to avoid passing what people say through your own judgment filter, where you quietly decide what *you* think about the matter. You may decide someone is over or underreacting, or reacting in a way you wouldn't. You may start thinking about who the good guys and the bad guys are in the story, or quietly question the veracity of the version of events you're getting.

You may put on a scientist or investigator hat and try to solve the mystery, identify the villain or decide who's wrong and why, or what facts are missing. Or you may play nurse or mother and decide that the bad feelings are unacceptable and that it's your job to heal this person, cheer them up, or scold them for making you unhappy...

But all of this is irrelevant—because it's about *you* and not about *them*. Your take on the matter doesn't matter right now. Suspend all your preconceptions and ideas and beliefs and immerse yourself in their world. How does it actually feel to be them right now? Don't merely picture yourself as you are in their situation—picture this person in their situation.

Another good idea is to give plenty of time for the person to speak and express, without hurrying the conversation along to a conclusion or summary. Even done subtly, this can feel like the listener wants to be done with the conversation quickly, and can really invalidate one's feelings. When someone shares their feelings with you and you respond with a simplistic summary, you're telling them that you're not available to listen further, and that what you really want is for them to stop feeling how they feel and get on with it.

Don't run ahead in the conversation or try to insert an interpretation, conclusion or solution before the speaker actually arrives there on their own time. This will communicate that you genuinely care. Let your speaker set the tone and pace, and match it empathetically. If you ask open-ended questions or merely reflect or show support, the person is likely to feel heard, whereas closed questions can feel like you're more interested in pushing the speaker down a particular path than letting them express what they are feeling.

You may never realize all the ways you subtly communicate to others that you don't in fact value their emotional experience and are not truly listening, even if you're trying really hard to be a better listener. Sometimes we don't even know all the ways we enter a dialogue with fixed ideas of how it should go, what the other person should say—and indeed the role we should play for them. You've probably been at the mercy of someone who truly believed they were being a "good listener," but you actually felt like your experience was merely being shoehorned into theirs.

A good listener is above all open and receptive, and unafraid to completely embrace another person's reality, entering alongside them in their feelings, whatever they are, without their own egos getting in the way. When you think about it, this phenomenon is so rare in the world today that if you can successfully demonstrate it to someone in a moment of vulnerability, you'll likely win their trust forever and significantly strengthen that relationship.

When in doubt, remember all the times you've wanted to talk and share your emotional world with someone else. At the time, did you want to hear their pop-psychology interpretation? Did you want to know their opinion on what you're doing wrong and how to fix it? Did you want them to freak out and get awkward, so you feel guilty for making *them* feel bad? Did you want them to "fact check" your story, or tell you you were overreacting, or side with someone else? Or would you have immensely appreciated it if they simply told you, "Hey, whatever happens, I'm here and I support you. Tell me more"?

Validate

When we think about empathy, withholding judgment, and simply ceding the floor to others, once again, it's not a completely passive activity.

Just like active listening, this process of making people feel heard contains several different layers. **Validation** is the verbal affirmation and acceptance of the emotions and viewpoints of someone we're communicating with. For our purposes, it's truly an extension of deep listening and being mindful of both the conversation and the meta-conversation that is occurring in front of us.

Normal listening takes care of the conscious conversation level, but validation satisfies an emotional need (the meta-conversation) that is presented any time anyone opens their mouth.

At first glance, validation might seem like a fairly simple concept of nodding and saying yes when people want you to (not very distinguishable from active listening, even), but even though it sounds relatively uncomplicated, there are right and wrong ways to validate.

Validation is one of the more powerful give-and-take practices of communication because it establishes respect between two people, whether they're old friends or strangers. Shutting down someone's feelings—even if they're repellant to us—effectively closes those floodgates off and isolates *both* sides of the exchange, putting the relationship at risk.

Genuine validation, on the other hand, helps everybody in the communication process score a win. The receiver gets a confirmation of their humanity, but the giver also enriches their own stature and enhances their sense of self-worth. Generosity, trust, and eagerness to confide emerge, and communication rarely goes wrong when all those elements are working.

Studies summarized in a 2010 article from the University of Rochester highlighted the positive and subtle effects the act of validation has in a successful relationship. It's not just a way of paying attention to people or showing respect for people's wishes. That is the lowest-hanging fruit that needs to be picked, but true validation goes far deeper in making people feel embraced and heard.

In one study, a selection of participants was instructed to concentrate on the best experience they'd had in the previous three years. Then they were matched with another person and encouraged to tell them about that experience. Unbeknownst to them, that other person was not a subject in the study but someone (a "confederate," as the researchers put it) who'd been trained to respond in a favorable way to their experience.

Other participants in the study were matched with confederates under the pretense that they too were just participants in the study. Instead of talking about their positive experience, though, they participated in a "fun" activity that involved drawing.

The feedback from the respondents after the third experiment showed an interesting split. Subjects who took part in the fun activity reported liking their partners more and that they'd enjoyed their time with them more than those who'd only spoken with them. But those who had discussed their experience and gotten a supportive response reported that they *trusted* the other person more and that they were more likely to be open with their private thoughts and feelings with those confederates.

These affirmations caused test subjects to feel even better about their positive experiences. They felt more assured about the daily, basic structures of their lives and generated a large amount of goodwill in return. They got another level of satisfaction and value on top of the original experience—all from a somewhat simple act of validation.

It's important to note that the positive events the subjects were talking about were not all major milestones that are commonly validated on a mass level—positive life-changers like graduation, marriage, or childbirth. Most of them were simply happy experiences or interactions, things that take place every day. But the validation of these smaller events was just as significant to the subjects, if not more. Hearing supportive remarks about them fostered conditions of trust and confidence, not to mention generosity in return.

Two-Step Emotions

Any verbal interaction looks simple on paper, but sometimes we can get tripped up on execution. Validation is no different: there are components one must include to make it felt. When someone confides in us or expresses a certain immediate emotion, they're looking to have that emotion processed and accepted by whomever they're talking with. That doesn't always happen.

There are two main components of an act of validation that define its success.

Identifying the emotion. While recognizing our own emotions is a crucial part of our personal mental health, being able to do so with someone else is a big plus in our relationships and social health. The ability to verbalize our interpretation of our partner's emotions—*before* they have to come right out and say "I'm angry" or "I'm sad"—opens the door to a positive validation. It shows that we're keyed in on what they're communicating, that we're really listening and not just hearing.

Justifying the emotion. Once we've identified what our communication partner is feeling, the next step is proclaiming it as a proper—or at least very understandable—emotional reaction: "Why, if *I* was in your shoes, I'd feel the same way too!" This establishes a sense of commonality, that our partner's sentiments are exactly what rational people would feel under the circumstances. It communicates that you are feeling the same emotion they are and emphasizes that the way they feel and think is justified.

Justifying your partner's feelings is a much more important component than instantly offering advice on what to do. They want to feel that you empathize with their plight first, before hearing what corrective measures they should take.

Without first acknowledging their emotions, even well-intentioned or accurate advice would simply infer that the speaker has been doing something wrong or that their emotional status is primarily their fault. Before giving advice, we need to connect with them on a sympathetic, emotional level. That will make working through a solution much easier and more supportive later. Oftentimes the act of validation, not advice, is really what people are seeking in an interaction.

This tells us emotional support is more important than having a to-do list to fix someone's circumstances or feelings; indeed, feeling better about something is *far more* important than knowing what to do about it.

How do these two components work in real communication? Let's first imagine a scenario that *doesn't* work:

> *Partner 1:* "I can't believe this! I'm getting heat at work for something my boss told me to do! I knew it was a bad idea, I protested it, they forced me to do it, it messed things up royally, and now my boss told me I'd have to work overtime this weekend to put everything back the way it was!"

Partner 2: "I told you that place was a disaster before you took the job. You shouldn't be surprised this is happening."

Partner 1: "Gee, thanks for making me feel worse."

Partner 2: "I'm not the one who wanted to go into the funeral home business. Don't look at me. Why don't you look for another job?"

What's wrong with Partner 2's response? Just about everything. Partner 1 was upset at what they perceived as an unfair situation. They felt upset that they weren't taken seriously at work and then got shafted when things went wrong. Partner 2 is essentially doing the exact same thing. By reminding Partner 1 that "I told you so," Partner 2 isn't taking their feelings seriously either. They judge Partner 1 for making the wrong choice to begin with and imply they shouldn't feel upset because, essentially, they made their bed and have to lie in it.

This exchange is much more on the mark:

Partner 1: "I can't believe this! I'm getting heat at work for something my boss told me to do! I knew it was a bad idea, I protested it, they forced me to do it, it messed things up royally, and now my boss told me I'd have to work overtime this weekend to put everything back the way it was!"

Partner 2: "Did they really do that? No! That's infuriating! I'd be livid about it too."

Partner 1: "I just feel like I don't have any control over my own destiny at that place."

Partner 2: "That must be really disheartening. I don't see how anyone would feel otherwise under such conditions, especially at a funeral home."

In that exchange, Partner 2 does a much better job of validating Partner 1's experience. They've identified the emotion Partner 1 is feeling, namely fury ("That's infuriating!"). They then established the emotion as proper or understandable and exactly the way people would feel in that situation ("I'd be livid about it too"). Partner 2 then repeats the process in the last statement: Partner 1 feels "disheartened," and anyone in those circumstances would feel and act the same.

Note that in the second exchange Partner 2 does not try to fix the problem or even necessarily take deliberate steps to make Partner 1 feel *that* much better. Partner 1 needs to feel enraged at the moment; it's a justifiable emotion. If Partner 2 had tried to force a solution by giving advice or suggesting something else, it would have interrupted Partner 1's emotional process. It would have been an effort to stop Partner 1 from feeling how they're entirely entitled to feel.

What's more important is that Partner 1 feels validated in their response, that they're understood and empathized with. That reinforces the quality of their communication. If there happens to be a way Partner 2 can effectively offer help or work through a solution later, great. But without a sense that the partner's feelings are valid, that effort won't amount to much. Even if you know what must be done and think someone is idiotic for engaging in self-defeating behaviors, think of it this way: they can't understand it unless they hear themselves say it. So you must humor them and engage in a certain degree of their drama to successfully validate and guide them toward emotional support and perhaps even a solution.

Validating Responses

In the first example above, Partner 2's responses are inappropriate because they derail Partner 1's legitimate emotions. Partner 2 doesn't want to spend time focusing on Partner 1 for whatever reason—they just don't want to deal with them. So Partner 2's ill-mannered, terse, and mean reaction makes a bad situation worse.

But not all such responses are meant in a bad way—one can also, unsuspectingly, invalidate someone's feelings with good intentions. Some of the more innocuous responses we give to someone's emotional tumult can actually hurt them without us realizing what's going on. This is likely what most of us are doing when we *think* we're validating; in fact, we're making the situation worse.

For example, when consoling someone over a situation that makes them nervous or apprehensive, one might say something like "*Don't worry about it*" or "*You shouldn't feel that way.*" And they might say it in a comforting tone to make them feel better. They mean well.

But such responses are actually invalidating. They *are* worried about their situation; they *already* feel that way. Telling someone they're not acting in the optimal way negates their entitlement to their own feelings. Even if you're making that remark out of kindness, your partner may receive it as invalidation of their perfectly normal feelings. It's simply unhelpful to hear, similar to telling someone, "*Hey, just grow taller.*"

An alternative response that successfully validates the other partner might be "*I can sense that you're worried about this situation."* This response assures the partner that their concerns are real and that their presence is reasonable. Remember, your goal is to identify emotions and then justify them—nothing more.

Another invalidating and unhelpful response is *"I'm sorry you feel that way."* You might think the phrase "I'm sorry" is a form of empathy. And in a way it can be. But it can also be interpreted as an empty sentiment. If someone's lost their job, been evicted, come down with a debilitating disease, or suffered some other awful injury or fate, "I'm sorry" doesn't quite cut it. By saying you're sorry someone is undergoing emotional turmoil—that they "feel that way"—you're also suggesting that there's a different way they *should* feel, but they're not. Whether they *should* feel a certain way is irrelevant, as they can't change what they already feel.

A more validating option would be *"I can understand why you're feeling this way—I think anyone else would too."* Explaining that they have a right to be uneasy and that such feelings are normal help relax tension and produce a bond with the rest of the world: they wouldn't be alone in feeling this way. Even if you think you *wouldn't* feel this exact way, it's important to establish that others *would*. (Besides, you might not really know how you would feel in this situation—it probably hasn't happened to you yet.)

Likewise, responses like *"At least it's not like…"* or *"It could be worse"* imply that your partner's concerns are illogical or unfounded. Emotions are never logical, but they *are* real. Maybe the issue *can* be worse, but not right in someone's subjective sense of reality. Objective comparisons to more dire situations serve to put the worrier "in their place," even if they're meant to make the partner feel better in the short term. But they're just friendlier forms of marginalization. The judgment as to whether someone's situation can or can't be worse belongs to the person who's feeling the emotions.

In this situation, a proper validating response would make the listener feel that they're being taken seriously: *"You've really been through a lot"* or *"Tell me more about what you're feeling."* These responses acknowledge the weight of the other person's issues, reassuring them that you're willing to take their worries seriously and don't want to minimize how badly they feel.

Outright rejections are not just invalidations but straight-up reproaches: *"I'm not having this discussion!"* This is invalidating because it directly cuts off communication and further says that the other person's concerns are unworthy. By saying this, the respondent imposes a limit on communication—obviously there are some subjects they're unwilling to discuss with you, when a true friend or partner wouldn't have any hands-off topics whatsoever.

A better response is *"Would you like some help working through this problem?"* or (again) *"Tell me more about what you're feeling."* This helps the partner feel like they have, if not a total solution, then at least an open path to finding a better result.

If it sounds like I'm suggesting you walk on eggshells when you're dealing with other people's feelings and one of these responses slips out, don't. You will make one of those responses again when you're done with this book. So will I, to be honest, because you and I both mean well, and we are humans who make mistakes. But be aware that those responses are invalidations that should be followed up as quickly as possible with validating statements. Remember that you're trying to form a connection and allow communication to flow freely. That will make the pivot back to validation easier to make.

Six Steps to Validation

Learning the six steps of validation as outlined by Kate Thieda might be a prudent place to start for those of us who like breaking down things into steps. When your friend or loved one is in a vulnerable state and is reaching out, these are the stages and the order you should go through to effectively hear and communicate with them.

1. Be present. First of all, show up. This is at once the easiest yet trickiest step of all. It doesn't mean just being physically present and maintaining eye contact. Being present is actually more like two smaller steps: giving your partner your absolute attention, then being accommodating and understanding that they're dealing with big emotions at the moment.

The first part is physical: it just means eliminating distractions. Turn off your phone, switch off the TV, and reduce the volume of music to a hum in the background. (You could also just turn it off, but relaxing music can make the environment for communication a little easier.) This is obviously more complicated in a public place—if it's easy to move to a quieter spot, do so. If not, try to ward off distractions by keeping complete visual focus on your partner and leaning in to hear if you have to.

The second part means accepting your partner's strong feelings—showing up in a sensitive way. We can react too quickly to a display of intense emotion, and it's fair to feel initially startled when someone's severely sad or angry. As soon as the shock recedes, though, it's crucial to let your partner know you want to deal with them as they are. You can do this by asking an open-ended question: *"Tell me what's going on,"* *"What are you feeling right now?"* or *"Can you talk about what happened?"* You should also watch and soften your visual and facial cues to let your partner know you're open to hearing and not ready to judge.

2. Accurate reflection. After you've listened to your partner explain what's happening, the next step is to show that you're concentrating on their well-being and trying to understand what they're feeling. That's when you attempt to offer an accurate reflection of what they've just expressed. Reflection can take different forms, but they are all verbal statements that mirror the emotions your partner is conveying, provide context, and assure them that you comprehend their feelings. *"I sense that you're disappointed about not getting that job"* or *"I can hear your anxiety about having to deal with your family at Thanksgiving."*

It doesn't have to be more than a sentence or two of acknowledgment—in fact, it shouldn't be. It should be just enough to let your partner know that you're hearing them, that you've invested your interest and concern, and want to hear them continue their story.

Also try to paraphrase their feelings in your own words instead of just repeating what they've said to you word for word. Simply echoing their statements verbatim only proves that you have a good short-term memory. Rephrasing it in your own language, though, shows that you're trying to *understand* them on a deeper level. (Plus, parroting something back to someone could be mistaken for sarcasm, like an adult mimicking a crying child.)

3. Reading behavior and guessing what they're feeling. For a variety of reasons, many of us are detached from and out of touch with our emotions. A big cause of this separation is having experienced invalidation in the past. Our parents may have neglected our feelings as kids (like that mimicking parent does in the last paragraph, for example). Or perhaps we've tried to be honest about our feelings with others before, and their reactions were so harmful that now we repress our emotions and keep them buried.

That's why the next step is guessing how your partner feels by how they're behaving: *"I'm guessing you're feeling rejected by your parents because they're not showing confidence in your decisions"* or *"It sounds to me like you're frustrated with your coworker because they're not keeping their commitments."*

It's vital to frame this statement as a *guess*, not a firm declaration of your belief or diagnosis of the situation. Being assertive puts you in a position where you're superior to the other person and you know the answers to their problems. That creates a distance, a sort of mentor-student relationship that might make your conversation partner less forthcoming, not to mention resentful. This is a step beyond reflecting emotions, because you aren't waiting for the other person to express themselves. You are taking the lead here and trying to guide them to an emotional resolution.

Another reason you need to present your interpretation of their feelings as a guess is, of course, that you might be wrong. In this step, being wrong is completely okay. You're trying to figure out what their emotions are. But ultimately, they're the ones who are feeling their emotions, and they know best what those are. If you supposed wrong, they might correct you. That, too, is completely okay. Give them a safe environment to explain themselves. If they know you're just speculating, they'll feel more secure in clarifying what's happening with them.

4. Understand their behavior in the context of their lives. This step depends on your having knowledge of your partner's past history and general makeup—and if you've been close for a long time, you should know that history reasonably well. All the reactions we have now are the product of events and experiences that we had in the past, as well as the way we're biologically constructed. In this validation step, you express a connection with their behavior by understanding how the past has shaped their actions and feelings.

For example, let's say your friend was hit by a car while he or she was riding their bike as a child. The injuries weren't serious but the event was understandably traumatic. Particularly since it happened when they were very young and impressionable, they may feel fearful about getting on a bike or crossing the street in heavy traffic.

That's a somewhat simple example in which everyone turned out relatively okay in the end (though it sucked at the time). But be aware there are many more serious and painful experiences for your partner that may be at play. They may have endured abuse, suffered from the early death of their parents, seen terrible violence in wartime or combat, or some other intense tragedy. You should tread with care in these instances—and your response should reflect that care. *"Knowing how you lost your mother at an early age, I think I understand why you're afraid of abandonment." "I imagine you can't easily trust someone after being in that abusive relationship."*

5. Normalize or affirm their emotional reactions. When something happens that causes a big reaction in us, it's a unique and new event—it's not a normal occurrence. It causes us to feel something we don't often experience in the usual course of our lives. But it's important to validate that emotion. Although the situation itself isn't normal, our partner's emotional reactions to that unusual situation are entirely normal.

For example, getting fired from a job isn't a small issue. It's a rare happening that can cause a lot of extreme stress and trauma. Someone who just got fired may be feeling anxious and worried for their future—and it's very important for them to know that anxiety and worry are completely proper things to feel. *"If I just got laid off, I'd feel nervous about the future too."* Your partner must understand that their reactions are not bizarre or wrong; they need to know that others would feel the same way if they were going through it.

However, when affirming their feelings as normal, it's important to *not* say something like *"You'll be fine"* or *"It's gonna be okay."* Those statements, well-intended as they are, actually invalidate your partner's feelings by effectively ending the discussion, negating the effect of their difficult emotions. You actually *don't* know if it's going to be fine. Even if your historical experiences with those feelings have turned out to be okay, that doesn't mean *theirs* will.

A preferable option would be *"I have faith in your ability to get through this"*—but even that's not completely necessary at this point. Your partner's feelings should be center stage. And they have to know that they are. Your being able to comprehend and validate how they feel is much more important to them right now. They need the space to complete that expression on their own without getting cut off by a nice sentiment that means well.

6. Radical genuineness. This is related to the previous stage of normalizing your partner's feelings and goes a step further. At the end of your communication, your partner should feel that they're a real person experiencing valid feelings and *not* like someone who's crazy and incompetent. Your endgame should result in your partner feeling loved and taken seriously—that you respect them as your equal, and they're just going through an exceptionally hard time at the moment.

This might be a good time for the expression *"I have faith you'll get through this,"* since it relates to their being a normal person in a challenging situation. But it's important to establish that *you* believe them to be that way—that you know they're able to solve their problems or adapt to changes, that they're not helpless or unable to make anything right. This is the definition of radical genuineness: treating and supporting your loved one as a human being that you trust and believe in, especially when they're down.

Relationships and friendships emerge from feelings of love, happiness, and satisfaction. But they're *preserved* by shaping those sentiments into practicing validation, and that takes work and conscientiousness.

Takeaways:

- Get into the hole with others—the holes that they have dug, not the one that you are digging beside them. Validation is a somewhat lost art. Validation is the act of showing respect and acknowledgment of people's intentions and emotions. It can be as easy as nodding your head, but it accomplishes the greater purpose of making people feel emotionally heard and fulfilled. At the most basic level, it consists of identifying people's emotions and then justifying them. You first act as a detective to understand what you are dealing with, and then make people feel that they are completely reasonable in their emotional experience. Emotions are never quite rational, but they are always real.

- Many times when we try to validate, we actually worsen the situation by using invalidating statements. These are statements that dismiss or minimize people's feelings, such as "Oh, you'll be fine" or "You shouldn't feel that way!" They're prescriptive and try to convince people to see the bright side of things—but that's not what they are in need of at the moment.

- A helpful six-step path to validation is as follows: being present, accurately reflecting emotions, guessing emotions, understanding emotions in context, affirming emotions, and then being honest.

Chapter 5. Read and Analyze

Listening is really an exercise in reading people, isn't it? You are taking in information and then making as accurate as assessment as you can.

There are ways to be a little more direct about this. In reality, deep listening is a subset of the skill of evaluating others. However, the common theme still remains of removing your own biases, desires, and goals from the equation. If you can't achieve this first goal, you will set yourself up for interpersonal failure.

The first way that we can generally read and analyze people better is through emotional intelligence.

Emotional Genius

The best modern conception of emotional intelligence comes from psychologist Daniel Goleman.

Emotional intelligence is knowing and perceiving the emotions you feel and why you feel them, then transferring that type of awareness onto others. You are able to put a label on your emotional state and find its cause and effect. By extension, emotional intelligence is being able to read other people's emotions accurately and deduce the reasons for them.

When you start thinking "Why did she say that?" and "What made him do that?" instead of immediately reacting, that's the beginning of your path to emotional intelligence. It's a matter of understanding the whole causal chain of other people's motivations and intentions and how that leads to their emotions, which lead to their behaviors.

High emotional intelligence is like being able to read someone's mind. In reality, this everyday superpower is not so complex and requires resisting powerful aspects of human nature that behoove us to focus only on ourselves.

Take Charlotte. Charlotte prances into the office, her steps lilting and a smile on her face. Before sitting down, she asks her coworker a question: "What do you think of my new haircut?" Derek, her coworker, doesn't care what her hair looks like whatsoever, but he likes Charlotte, and he also knows that she often worries about her looks. "It looks great," he enthuses. "The new cut really brings out your eyes."

"I thought so too!" she gushes, taking her seat. "Thanks." She smiles.

Because Derek understood and cared about Charlotte's emotions, he knew she was asking for encouragement and praise rather than an apathetic dismissal. He read the situation and connected to her emotional state rather than to her simple and seemingly innocent question. His kind response bolstered her impression of his trustworthiness and kindness, raising her opinion of him.

Every time you improve your emotional intelligence, you'll have more interactions like these. It's about understanding and consideration and stepping outside of your own desires and perspectives. Daniel Goleman's modern conception of emotional intelligence can be described in four major categories. They all work together to create a blueprint for understanding and reading others more effectively.

Self-Awareness

When we're self-aware, we know who we are, what we think, and what we feel. We know that when we get depressed, we'll get less done. We know that when we drink coffee, we tend to be peppier and more productive. We understand that when we're feeling stressed, we're less likely to have patience for other people's needs. We recognize emotion as an underlying basis for most of our actions.

In short, we have knowledge of what we feel, why we feel that way, and how our feelings will impact our behavior. Self-aware people are also able to observe the effects their emotions have on other people. Happiness and sadness alike tend to be contagious, and a self-aware person will know that their emotions impact and are impacted by their environment.

Self-awareness also involves knowing our strengths and knowing weaknesses. More importantly, it helps us be willing and able to accept advice and criticism. People who aren't as aware of their real skills or value will either think they're too incompetent and incapable of learning or that they already know everything and don't need to be taught.

Neither is true of anyone, and people who fall into those traps come off as lazy or as arrogant know-it-alls, respectively. When you can admit you need help and accept the help or advice offered, you show other people that you value their opinion and respect their knowledge. Accepting help makes the people helping you feel important and needed, which is something we all appreciate. Stop thinking about your faults as bad things; they're really opportunities to make friends and learn new things.

You can improve your self-awareness in a lot of ways. Overall, you just need to know yourself better. Professional-level psychological or personality tests can give some insight, as can asking your friends to rate you on various personality traits or skills. It's also possible to watch how people respond to you when you do or say certain things and gain insight about what traits you have that contribute to their reactions.

Or you can simply sit and reflect upon things you've done and ask *why*. And then ask *why* again. And then do it three more times—this typically allows you to cut through the defenses you've constructed around yourself and get to the heart of matters. Anything that gives you feedback about why you feel your emotions is useful.

Take a step back and pause whenever you experience a strong emotion. Close your eyes and try to trace what happened in the past hour or two that led you to feel that way. Are there any facts or experiences in the past that would explain why you feel a particular way about certain things and people in your life? What is currently casting a subconscious shadow over your mood?

For example, if you're angry at 6:00 p.m., start thinking about what you've done since 3:00 p.m. You've driven home, had a snack, changed into your sweatpants, and watched a little bit of television.

When you visualize your drive home, though, suddenly you remember that you were cut off by somebody and that you were beeped at incessantly. This agitated you and you were still feeling the effects of that mood dampener hours later. This is a simplification of the process that begins to take place much more instantly.

The sad reality is that most people are not in tune with their feelings. Often, we are negatively affected by the emotional impact of things that have long since been irrelevant. Most people just react automatically without realizing why and without stopping to think what is happening internally. They fall into patterns that are sometimes negative and sometimes destructive.

Rather than looking inward and attempting to label your emotions based on what you might hypothesize caused them, you can also analyze how you are acting and label them that way. In the former, you are looking to the past to try to deduce a cause. In the latter, you are looking at the present to see the manifestation of emotion. In a sense, you are working backward from what you see and creating at least one theory about what caused it.

Just as with other people, you can tell more about yourself by your actions than you can by what you say (or what you tell yourself).

Self-Management

The most fundamental aspect of self-management is the ability to keep our emotions in check. When we're ecstatic because we got a date with a dreamboat, we don't let that excitement distract others in business meetings. When we're angry about being overlooked for a promotion, we don't let that impact our work relationship with our rival or our boss.

We even work to stay calm, steady, and effective when situations are stressful, hostile, or dangerous. In short, it involves not letting emotions get the best of you.

A lot of people attempt to do this by bottling up their emotions, but that's a bad idea because it can lead to resentment, bitterness, and even eventual explosions of hatred and rage. Our emotions help us understand what we really think about events and people. Paying attention to them can let us form rational descriptions of our concerns and joys that can let us impact our work and relationships in positive ways. Notice what you feel, examine why you feel it, and talk about it calmly with relevant parties when your head is clear. That will let you form meaningful compromises and help you gain more happiness in life. In short, express emotions in appropriate, productive ways; don't repress them. This step is the next step in being self-aware: what do you actually *do* with your emotions that you've identified?

Self-management also involves monitoring our thoughts and moods to manufacture a positive outlook. Some people are natural optimists, some aren't, but seeking out the opportunities and lessons in even the worst situations can produce a silver lining that allows for meaningful growth and progress. You can't let yourself be crushed by a failure; you have to push through it, learn everything it taught you by heart, and do better next time. A well-managed emotional life is used to motivate you toward your goals because you can use conscious patterns of optimistic thought to rally yourself with hope and joy, letting you continue on your journey. Everyone likes people who can encourage them to go on in the face of hardship, and developing this optimism will do exactly that.

The final trait in self-management is flexibility. A lot of people become attached to doing things a certain way and balk when a better method comes along. Others are so scared of change that they presume anything new must be bad. But a self-managed person will see those impulses as unhelpful and try to learn new ways of thinking and doing things. This helps them adapt and manage their expectations and emotions better.

Self-Motivation

Arguably a subset of self-management, self-motivation pushes people to meet and exceed expectations—because they know what emotions they want more and less of. They have a good guess on what will make them feel fulfilled, and they try to accomplish that constantly.

Self-motivated people continually look for ways to improve their emotional state. They know what makes them tick, emotionally and otherwise, and try to set themselves up for success. You can supercharge your ability to do this by noticing when you or others complain. Complaints indicate problems, which are opportunities for improvement. When you find these, think about ways to solve the problem, and when you can make those solutions happen, get to it!

Social Awareness

People who are socially aware can read the room and understand the emotions that groups and individuals are likely feeling.

At a group level, being socially aware means understanding the power structure and organization of groups, along with the emotional impact of those structures and the emotional currents that flow between one person and the next. It helps us interpret situations. Understanding that the secretary is happy to help her boss but is tired from overwork is part of social awareness.

It's also social awareness to know that she's more replaceable and therefore less important and that both she and her boss are influenced by that dynamic. It sounds like an overwhelming amount of data to process, but it can be simplified to asking why people have certain behaviors with one person versus another and then finding the dynamic that causes it.

Observing and interacting with people helps develop this skill. Whenever you see an interaction that puzzles or intrigues you, you can ask yourself why they're saying and doing what they are to try to get a better grasp of relationship dynamics. The better you get, the easier it will be to find the right things to do in social situations of every size and type. Obviously, this is a massive oversimplification, but it begins with asking why something is happening and what unseen or unconscious elements are causing it.

Ask yourself these questions, one at a time at first, and shortly they will become instinctual habit. It's not an easy task because you can't focus on one factor definitively. Each situation is different, and you must be adaptable in discovering why people feel what they do. Going through this checklist will assist you in reading people's emotions in a way you may never have considered before.

- How might your thoughts and actions be misinterpreted?
- What are other people's primary motivations and what unspoken, underlying motivations might they have that they (and you) are not even aware of?
- Consider people's built-in biases and life circumstances that give rise to certain emotions. What is their background and upbringing?
- How do people display their emotions both positively and negatively?
- How are emotions displayed in different ways?
- What emotions are they likely to be feeling and why?
- What is the purpose for what they are saying?
- What is their baseline emotional state and preferred interaction style?

By being aware of these factors, you increase your emotional intelligence because you are able to read people more accurately. And just as important, you can respond to them in a more calibrated manner that leads to fewer negative reactions. Notably, this process can take a while—exactly the difference between responding and reacting.

At the most basic level, emotional intelligence is knowing the range of reactions to any given statement or circumstance and who might respond differently and why.

If you insult someone's mother in a serious manner and with a serious face, one reaction would be anger and being offended. You can expect that reaction a majority of the time. However, what are the other possible reactions, and what accounts for the difference? People might assume you are joking, laugh out of confusion, or ignore you because they didn't even hear what you said.

Emotional intelligence will allow you to connect with people on a deeper level because you understand them implicitly without their saying anything. You will just get them. This is what many people interpret as chemistry and rapport, and you will have it in a seemingly effortless manner.

You can see how emotional intelligence starts from yourself and then transfers to others. In the previous chapter, we focused a lot on values and deeper intentions, which inform how people would like to act. Here, we are paying more attention to emotions, which tells you how they will more naturally and instinctually act. Taken together, we are learning how to analyze someone's rational and emotional sides to both predict their behavior and also interpret it.

A final and important piece of emotional cues is to get better at understanding the subtext of a situation, which is similar to social awareness.

That's Not What I Meant!

Communication is much more than the words that we speak or hear. Studies have quoted figures stating that 50% to 90% of communication—the message and emotion we get from others—is based on nonverbal or unspoken signals, starting from Mehrabian and Ferris in "Inference of Attitudes from Nonverbal Communications in Two Channels" in 1967. Add that to additional communication based on subtext, context, implication, and inference, and you'll almost wonder what impact our actual words have.

Whatever the case, what we think we are communicating is often overshadowed or outright contradicted by what is meant to be interpreted between the lines. What we say is not really what we mean most of the time, and this is something we begin to learn as children. It's not that the words we use don't matter—they do. But the way in which we use them, and the contexts we use them in, are far more indicative of our feelings and emotions.

Unfortunately, for many of us, these small signs might as well be incantations for magic spells based on how subtle or convoluted they seem. One of the keys to communicating more clearly and being able to read between the lines of what people say is to understand *subtext*. To borrow from Chaney and Lyden's 1997 publication "Subtextual Communication Impression Management: An Empirical Study," in the context of an office environment, subtext is the following:

> Subtextual communication, a covert language that strengthens or negates the spoken text, is used to influence the impressions other people have of us and may be used to competitive advantage in numerous situations in the workplace. The subtext is more subtle than the obvious text and may be more honest in interactions between people (Fast, 1991).
>
> Subtextual communication elements are related to image and may convey positive or negative impressions related to assurance, credibility, competence, and savoir-faire through dress, manner of introducing people, body language, regard for time, use of electronic communication, and dining etiquette.

Paul got a part-time job to give him extra cash as he got his university degree. He decided to work in a local electronics store because he knew the people, the area, and the product like the back of his hand. Imagine his surprise when he discovered he wasn't the big sales star he made himself out to be during the interview process.

Everyone else seemed to hit their sales quotas with ease, yet there he was, stuck barely reaching the lower end of the target. What made matters worse was the fact that other staff members had absolutely no technical knowledge, yet they surpassed Paul in sales every single month.

Paul's sales were so bad that his boss called him in for a performance meeting to address the problem. Instead of pointing out where Paul went wrong, he decided to match him up with his top salesman to discover how the sales techniques differed.

For the entire afternoon, Paul tagged along with the top-performing salesperson, Sam. As Paul observed, he noticed something interesting. The customers were all completely the same, the queries were all the same, and his solutions were the same—except for one small thing.

Where Paul would give up or move on, Sam offered additional recommendations and moved in for the kill. He realized this when a customer was looking at a camera. The customer raised his hands and declared the product to be "fine." At this point, Sam picked up a more expensive camera and walked the customer through its features. Paul wouldn't usually do that—when the customer said something was "fine," he would continue focusing on closing the sale on the same camera.

But to his surprise, the customer ended up buying the more expensive camera. As soon as the customer left the store, Paul asked Sam, "What made you suggest a whole new product? Isn't that just confusing the customer? I thought he said it was fine!"

Sam just laughed and said, "Just because the customer says it's fine doesn't mean it is. Fine is not positive. It usually means they want something more or their expectations haven't been met. It's them asking for more options in reality."

Paul was taking people's words literally and only at face value, and because of that, he was missing the real messages people were sending him. Whatever was being said was the only thing Paul was operating on, and he didn't consider that communication would occur in any other way. Sam explained that people's words were merely the tip of the iceberg in terms of what they wanted to communicate, and "fine" said with a flat speaking tone was as good as "this sucks." That one simple statement made a huge change in Paul's sales, as he began trying to dig beneath the words themselves and pick up on the meaning behind them.

Don't be like Paul. Learn subtext to read people better and begin to truly respond to what people are trying to communicate.

Communication can be divided into two categories: overt and covert. Overt is the words we say and the explicit messages we want to convey. This is when we directly tell someone that we're hungry and ask for a hamburger.

Subtext is the covert type of communication. It's almost never directly said, relies on literally anything besides the direct message coming out of someone's mouth, and requires correct interpretation. Using subtext to say "I'm hungry" would include rubbing your stomach, licking your lips, pointing out that there is a menu on a nearby table, and mentioning that your previous meal was tiny.

Not everyone is going to pick up on those signs, but it is undeniable what the person wanted to convey. We routinely communicate through these indirect means and hope that it saves us the trouble of being direct. Subsequently, understanding the subtext under and surrounding people's seemingly benign statements gives you insight into their true feelings and thoughts.

For example, how does the overt dialogue below differ from the subtextual, covert message? Here, it's what is *not said* that completes the message. The subtext is that the question wasn't replied to in a convincing manner and, thus, is less than sincere. Suppose the answerer of the question has a history of being blunt.

"Am I fat?"
"No, you're not fat."
Translation: Yes, you might be a little bit fat.

"Am I fat?"
"No, but I suppose you could maybe lose a couple of pounds."
Translation: Yeah, you're definitely fat now.

Subtext can be delivered through vocal tone, phrasing, delivery, reference to prior experiences, knowledge of relationships, body language, gesticulation, circumstances, and even moods. It sounds abstract and confusing, but just imagine that subtext is everything we want to say besides the *exact words* we use.

In fact, that's one of the big reasons we use it. It allows us to navigate the world through indirect and nonconfrontational means. If you're great at subtext, it saves time, it's efficient, and it imparts great emotional intelligence by understanding people's ever-shifting circumstances.

Subtext appears in every situation, from work and dating to social situations and family dynamics. In fact, much of dating can be said to be subtext because much of sexual tension depends on not revealing true intentions up front. If you ask someone to dinner and they tell you they are busy, they might be busy, or they might not be interested. If you ask the same person out four times and each time they say they're busy, then there is additional subtext for you to read. Take the context into account and things aren't looking good for you on the romantic front.

Through our behavior and choice of words, we transmit clues and desperately hope people pick up on them. Of course, this is the origin of passive-aggressive behavior—we don't feel comfortable saying something directly, so our indirect measures become more and more aggressive and unpleasant. As a species, we are fairly avoidant and nonconfrontational. Not many people feel comfortable wearing their opinions and hearts on their sleeves, especially when they clash with those of other people. Directness is inherently tense, so it's something we prefer to avoid.

A helpful method to imagine how subtext works in social situations is to imagine how it factors into a novel or a screenplay. When you're watching a movie or reading a book, you don't usually get told what the characters understand, feel, or think, and despite that, you come away with a clear sense of meaning about the scenes and relationships. This is all because of subtext.

In this context, it's commonly referred to as what is *under the skin of the character*— what drives and motivates them, what they feel toward everyone else in the story, and what's under the surface of all of their actions. Without giving characters clear motivations and having everyone in the movie operate only on a "what you see is what you get" level, you end up with a flat movie with no emotional impact.

Even in movies, there can be ambiguity in the subtext—sometimes intentional and sometimes not. This is the part the audience must fill in, which is why two people can come out of a film and have radically different ideas about the meaning the director was trying to convey.

Let's take a look at an example scene in detail to illustrate this clearly. Always remember that we have to separate the covert and overt communication.

Imagine a room where a man clasps a tiny baby-blue box in his hands. The table is decorated with roses and Champagne. A woman appears at the side of the frame and prepares to leave the room. She does not notice the man in the corner. He says, "Wait!"

Why does the man call the woman?

If you say, "Because he wants to propose to her," you have understood the subtext present in this basic scene. The dialogue never says that the man wants to propose marriage to the woman. You inferred that from a combination of the mood, the description, and the scene itself.

Is the word "wait" subtext? In this scene, the man is telling the woman to stop. There is nothing hidden in his words other than "Don't go!" or perhaps "Stay!" depending on how the word is delivered.

Imagine instead that the man overtly says, "I have a table laid out here for you and I intend to propose with this beautiful ring I bought from Tiffany & Co." It's not something that would happen in real life, and thus, movies have to be written with subtext that allows people to understand what's happening.

Filling in the details of any incoming communication through subtext is integral to better communication and greater likability. If you look closely, you will soon find that almost everything a person says has shades of subtext meant to consciously or unconsciously communicate additional messages.

Pay attention to people's prior history and experiences and how they might relate to the current situation. What emotions are at play here? Hint: there is always at least one primary emotion at play. It will inevitably color their perspectives, priorities, and motivations in a way that could make their message differ from their words. If you know someone's general personality traits, you can often make a call by analyzing the situation from how they would prefer to conduct themselves. If someone is extremely meek and quiet and says something to the effect of "I agree… I suppose," then it probably means they are internally screaming "NO!" Essentially, consider the source and how a person's experiences color their communication.

Judge someone's authenticity by analyzing the tone of their voice. Are they angry, serious, or sarcastic? Does the tone match the message? If someone says yes but they use a sarcastic tone, then they probably mean no. If someone says yes but they are angry, then they are probably not happy with the outcome. If they are serious and they say yes, then they are conflicted or they probably don't care. There is a virtually unlimited number of interpretations of vocal tone, but most of them indeed mean that the words aren't meant to be taken at face value.

Observe how people respond to you. When you look at how patient people are, how nice they act, and how accommodating they try to be, you can gauge how they feel about what you say. This also extends to how much silence you hear and how much interest they show. If someone takes two beats to answer a simple question, they had to think about their reply and may be using subtext to communicate negativity even if they agree with you.

Another aspect to consider, which may require more intense observational skills, is to see how much they deviate from their usual pattern of behavior. If your supervisor is typically upbeat, what does it mean that they are somber and negative? It can turn a proclamation of "Things are going well..." into the exact opposite message.

Subtext leaves clues that you can harness to become an expert communicator. People leave signs everywhere.

Of course, the tough part is deciphering these aspects of people simultaneously and instantly, as you might do in a normal everyday conversation. This means you actually have two tasks: (1) processing the conversation and responding appropriately and (2) being on the lookout for subtextual cues. You might be able to train yourself to pick up on specific types of subtext and social cues, but can you pick up on them while trying to find others? Or will you only be able to observe so many things at once? It might seem like you'd need three brains and six pairs of eyes to pick up on so many things at once—at the beginning, this might be true.

But the only thing we can do is start small and train yourself until these things become a subconscious habit to consider—*why did they say that, what are they feeling, and what could it mean?*

I want to end the section on subtext with a small exercise to get you into the mood. It's fairly easy: go out into public and observe people interacting—for example, sitting at a café and covertly watching the people at nearby tables. You can't hear the overt conversation, so you're going to make a guess at the subtext of the covert communication. Assign backstories, emotions, and motivations to the people you are observing. Go out on a limb and make up stories. Once you get better at subtext, you'll find that the stories you create in situations like this will become more and more accurate.

Takeaways:

- We've talked about values and rational intentions that people might have. This chapter focuses on emotional cues that we can use to analyze people, and taken together, we are able to better predict and understand both rational and emotional states.
- Better understanding people's emotions begins with understanding your own. This comes in the form of emotional intelligence, and Daniel Goleman's conception of emotional intelligence consists of self-awareness (what do I feel and why), self-management (how

can I express my emotions safely and learn from them), self-motivation (what makes me happy, and how can I achieve that), and social awareness (what are other people feeling and why. The whole process begins with understanding yourself and then realizing that everyone else has the same amount of unconscious and hidden thoughts that dictate their emotions and actions. It is a way of thinking that must be trained and allows you to pull a significant amount of information from a small interaction.

- Likewise, we must learn to understand subtextual cues better. This is related to the social awareness element of emotional intelligence. We must realize that most communication is covert, and yet most of us are only responding to communication that is overt. This means we frequently miss the true meaning of people's words and actions. The easiest way to adopt this particular method of thinking is to ask, *why did they say that, what are they feeling, and what could it mean?*

Summary Guide

Chapter 1. One Mouth but Two Ears

- We've all got two ears but only one mouth, right? This means we should do about double the listening versus speaking, but the truth is doing so goes against our natural instinct. We are wired to express and talk about ourselves—to the extent that it provides the same type of neurological stimulation as sex. Fair enough, but that doesn't mean talking nonstop is acceptable or helpful to our relationships.
- It's time to view listening as the true win-win in cultivating deeper relationships. When you listen, you not only get to learn about someone, you are (paradoxically to some) seen as more charismatic, interesting, and enjoyable to interact with. So if your end goal is to be those things, listening is the skill you

must perfect. It's a simple skill, but certainly nothing close to easy.

- The challenge is that there are so many unconscious ways we wrest control over a conversation and become a conversational narcissist. This is simply when someone speaks so much that it appears to be a monologue versus a shared dialogue. One subtle way this occurs is through support versus shift responses, where the feeling you impart to others can hinge on a single vocabulary choice. The underlying theme, however, is to accept letting go of control, pride, and ego, and go wherever someone else wishes to go.

- A more conscious obstacle many people face is the feeling that the people they interact with are quite boring and have nothing worthwhile to say; thus, listening to them is not a good use of their time. Just reading that sentence, you should be able to spot a few flaws. If you think most people you run across are boring, you're the boring one. You're letting a prejudgment dictate your actions, and ruin your interactions. Instead, expect that you will find something fascinating and delightful, and that's just what will begin to happen.

- For a role model on how to draw information out of people, look no further than late-night talk-show hosts. Their sole job is to make a celebrity, often no funnier than you or I, appear immensely charming and intelligent. That's a tough task sometimes. Think about the energy, focus, attention, and listening they employ to make this happen. That's what is possible.

Chapter 2. Styles, Frames, and Levels

- Let's suppose you're trying to learn how to play the guitar. You're right-handed, but you've accidentally gone and bought a guitar for left-handers. This is not a recipe for success. That's how we can think about the different types of listening styles that exist. We must match our style with that of other people if we are to have any hope for success.

- Though it can be said there are countless listening styles, it's helpful to think in terms of four main styles: people (emotion), content (information), action (to-do list), and time (duration and frequency) orientations. For our purposes, we want to recognize which is our natural tendency, and then try to skew more toward the people/emotion style. This is because when people communicate outside of giving an order or organizing an outing, they are doing so to express an emotion. Go find it! Another way to delineate listening styles is to think in terms of head, heart, and hands. Head is all about thinking and planning, hands is all about doing and action, and the heart, well, that's all about emotion and people's well-being. Again, recognize where you are, and how to move toward people/emotion/heart styles of listening.

- Frames are a different way to imagine listening styles. Frames are much more fluid, and simply ask you to consider what someone's overall goals or purpose for the interaction is. What is theirs, what is yours, and do they match? If not, utilize your new understanding and make them match. An easy way to think about frames is in terms of an acting scene. All the actors are on the same page, working toward the same goal, and trying to capture an emotional payoff. What happens if one of the actors wants to wing it for a bit, and expound on their character's love of the sea? Nothing good.

- Finally, we get to levels of listening. Unlike listening frames and styles, some of these levels of listening are just plain bad. The levels are: ignoring, pretending to listen, selectively listening, attentively listening, and empathetically listening. The first two levels are not very useful, and it's only when we reach the ultimate level of empathetically listening that we remove ourselves from the equation and listen to hear rather than listen to reply. Most of us are stuck in the first three to four levels for the majority of our day-to-day interactions.

Chapter 3. The Tough Work of Hearing Someone

- Listening is a truly not a passive activity. Well, it can be, but that would just mean that you're not doing a good job. True, deep listening can be said to be extremely active, to the point of tiring you out! Surprised? This is because the purpose of true, deep listening is to *go there* with someone, and this involves teasing out exactly where you are even heading. It's a job that requires a lot of comprehension, solving subtle mysteries, and clarification. It's a bit like a therapist's role in helping unravel emotions and situations.

- To this end, we come to the concept of active listening. It's a way to participate in conversations while being on the receiving end. Most might think that receiving simply means sitting quietly, but that's a huge mistake. There are nine types of active listening responses we cover, to be used when trying to connect deeply with someone: comprehending, retaining, responding, restating, reflecting, summarizing, labeling emotions, probing with leading questions, and silence. The next level of active listening could be called empathetic reflection, and this is where the listener focuses on emotion, so much so that you are trying to predict what the speaker is feeling, and share it with them.

Chapter 4. I See You, I Hear You

- Get into the hole with others—the holes that they have dug, not the one that you are digging beside them. Validation is a somewhat lost art. Validation is the act of showing respect and acknowledgment of people's intentions and emotions. It can be as easy as nodding your head, but it accomplishes the greater purpose of making people feel emotionally heard and fulfilled. At the most basic level, it consists of identifying people's emotions and then justifying them. You first act as a detective to understand what you are dealing with, and then make people feel that they are completely reasonable in their emotional experience. Emotions are never quite rational, but they are always real.

- Many times when we try to validate, we actually worsen the situation by using invalidating statements. These are statements that dismiss or minimize people's feelings, such as "Oh, you'll be fine" or "You shouldn't feel that way!" They're prescriptive and try to convince people to see the bright side of things— but that's not what they are in need of at the moment.

- A helpful six-step path to validation is as follows: being present, accurately reflecting emotions, guessing emotions, understanding emotions in context, affirming emotions, and then being honest.

Chapter 5. Read and Analyze

- We've talked about values and rational intentions that people might have. This chapter focuses on emotional cues that we can use to analyze people, and taken together, we are able to better predict and understand both rational and emotional states.
- Better understanding people's emotions begins with understanding your own. This comes in the form of emotional

intelligence, and Daniel Goleman's conception of emotional intelligence consists of self-awareness (what do I feel and why), self-management (how can I express my emotions safely and learn from them), self-motivation (what makes me happy, and how can I achieve that), and social awareness (what are other people feeling and why. The whole process begins with understanding yourself and then realizing that everyone else has the same amount of unconscious and hidden thoughts that dictate their emotions and actions. It is a way of thinking that must be trained and allows you to pull a significant amount of information from a small interaction.

- Likewise, we must learn to understand subtextual cues better. This is related to the social awareness element of emotional intelligence. We must realize that most communication is covert, and yet most of us are only responding to communication that is overt. This means we frequently miss the true meaning of people's words and actions. The easiest way to adopt this particular method of thinking is to ask, *why did they say that, what are they feeling, and what could it mean?*

Lightning Source UK Ltd.
Milton Keynes UK
UKHW021936190722
406090UK00005B/230